The Autobiography of

GEORGE CHARLES PAGE

"The interesting thing about George is that he became very successful at making lots of money, then he became an expert at giving it all away!"

—*Art Linkletter*,
Chairman, Linkletter Enterprises

"Los Angeles County has benefitted immensely from George Page's philanthropic and cultural interests. His Page Museum is a crowning jewel in our cultural life."

—*Edmund D. Edelman*,
Supervisor

"Few who drive along Wilshire Boulevard and see his name on the museum monument sign realize that George C. Page, prominent businessman and philanthropist, began life as a poor, barefoot boy in a small town in Nebraska. He is an inspiration to multitudes."

—*Pat Boone*
Entertainer

"My dear friend, George page, at age 92 is the youngest man I know. He has accomplished so much in his lifetime of living the American dream. Like the hundreds of children he has rescued, he has maintained a child-like fresh view of the world—and it is a better place because of him."

—*June Haver MacMurray*,
Friend

The Life Story of

GEORGE CHARLES PAGE

In My Own Words

Written by him in longhand,
with the able assistance of
Catherine Corday Singer

Griffin Publishing
Glendale, California

ISBN 1-882180-12-7

Griffin Publishing
544 Colorado Street
Glendale, California 91204

Manufactured in the United States of America.

CONTENTS

County Supervisor Edmund D. Edelman
presenting George Page a scroll that
honors him for his civic interests

INTRODUCTION

One might wonder why a number of unrelated organizations—from Child-Help USA and Children's Hospital to Pepperdine University and the Los Angeles County Museum of Natural History—went to such great lengths to celebrate the 90th birthday of George Charles Page. The answer is, Mr. Page has led a life of unique adventures, successful business endeavors and unselfish service to humanity. He is a man who not only learned how to make millions, but also learned how to live a full and rewarding life as well. He is a rare combination of creativity and simplicity, ingenuity and humility, diligence and generosity. We are indebted to him for his contributions to life in Los Angeles and, now, for sharing his story with us in this volume.

Dr. Charles B. Runnels
Chancellor,
Pepperdine University
Malibu, California

My mother, Verna, holding me at age 3 months

CHAPTER ONE

I first saw the light of day in the town of Fremont, Nebraska, on June 25, 1901. My 17-year-old mother, Verna Siders Page, had made advance arrangements for a doctor to come to the house for the delivery, but when she needed him, he couldn't be located. In his place, a young doctor, fresh from medical school, arrived. But with his limited experience, he had no idea of how to turn a breech-birth baby. My mother had to endure a three-hour ordeal without anesthesia, and I was finally delivered the hard way.

I made no sound, so I was presumed dead and laid aside while the young doctor concentrated on trying to make my mother more comfortable. Later, I was noticed to move, so the surprised doctor lifted me up and applied the proverbial slap. In short order, I was quite conscious and announcing my arrival to the world. The doctor was paid the customary $10 for his services.

In those days, most babies were delivered in the home. Prenatal care was rare, and hospitals were considered unnecessary. Although anesthesiology was starting to be used, there were still those of certain religious groups who believed that women should suffer in childbirth to atone for Eve having given Adam the forbidden apple.

Mother was of English stock and was a high school graduate—not as common then as today. She had been reading about childbirth and was better informed than most women in rural Nebraska at that time.

My 22-year-old father, Fred Page, was of German and English ancestry and was very industrious. He started a hay contracting business, gradually adding equipment and horses. My parents purchased a two-story home and were getting along remarkably well for the limited opportunities in the little town of Fremont.

At the time of my birth, excitement over the new "automobile" was sweeping the nation. Originally, it was considered a rich man's toy. However, autos were beginning to make appearances on public streets in many places, causing horses to rear with fright. Also at this time, despite the general opinion that man would never fly, the Wright brothers created a contraption in their bicycle shop that eventually ascended and stayed aloft for 59 seconds. On December 17, 1903, the world's first flight-machine actually flew a distance of 852 feet!

When I was a baby, the popular song of the day was "Meet Me in St. Louis." It was inspired by the World's Fair in St. Louis, Missouri, which attracted more than 30 million visitors.

By the age of two, I'm told, I was "into everything." I would stack a box on my high chair and reach the cookie jar on the top shelf. It wasn't easy for my parents to conceal Christmas gifts in advance of the holidays. Somehow I would always find them.

When I was three, my mother gave birth to a second son, whom she named Harold. I was so accustomed to getting all the attention that it wasn't easy for me to adjust to taking second place. But in time, I was reconciled to the idea of a new family member and became very fond of my baby brother.

On Sundays, we boys were decked out in our Sunday best and taken to the Methodist Church for Sunday School. I didn't like to hear the compliments people paid regarding my little brother's blond curls. To pacify me, my mother bought me a cute little red leather cap. I well recall the day my little red cap blew off into a puddle of water. My father rescued the cap with a stick. And although Mother felt confident she could clean and salvage the cap, she remarked disgustedly, "What a pity your little cap is ruined"—whereupon I threw the cap back into the puddle.

"Why did you do that?" she demanded.

"Well, you said it was ruined, didn't you?" I replied in my little voice. After that experience, Mother was careful to be a bit more literal in what she said!

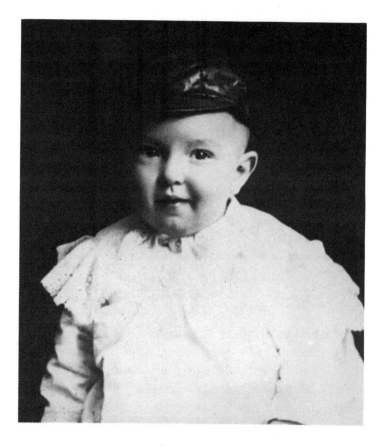

Me at age 3, with my little red cap

I had almost reached the age of five, and my brother three, when my father was seriously injured while inspecting a hay stacking machine. A heavy piece of equipment fell on him and broke his back. As a young man of 27 and in excellent health, he made a rapid recovery, and I can remember him up and around on crutches very quickly. However, blood poisoning set in a little later, and without the benefit of penicillin, he died. At the age of 22, my mother was left a widow with two little boys.

The proceeds from life insurance and the liquidation of my father's equipment and horses gave my mother a modest "nest egg." My grandparents suggested we move in with them, and my mother agreed. The house turned out to be a little small for all of us, so my mother paid for the building of an addition. But after it was completed, my grandfather began complaining that the noise we boys made caused him to be nervous. It wasn't long before Mother packed a suitcase following an argument, and we moved to a boardinghouse.

The owner of the boardinghouse gave my mother a part-time job in exchange for our room and board. Knowing how uncomfortable it was for us boys to be cooped up in a room all day, she decided she must make a change soon. The landlady had an unmarried brother about my mother's age, and in her eagerness to get us out of the boardinghouse and into a home of our own, Mother married the brother, John Tipton. She then rented a house at her expense, because Tipton had neither money nor a profession. Eventually, he got a job with a house mover earning two dollars a day. When it rained, he couldn't work, so there were weeks when his take-home pay was only six or eight dollars.

By today's standards, we were an "economic basket case." And in those so-called "good old days," there were no welfare agencies nor food stamps. Of course, we were too proud to admit we were "poor"—so we became very resourceful and managed on our own without help.

Mother learned from a neighbor how to buy men's blue serge trousers in the thrift shops: always look for the trousers with the biggest waist—the larger the better. Being less active, big men wear out the seat, but the material in the large trouser legs remains in good condition. By discarding the worn-out seat and salvaging the material in the legs, there was enough good material to sew and make pants for us boys. So, when school started, we appeared in our well-pressed, new pants with our self-respect and pride intact, despite being very poor!

Mother also learned to remodel and spruce-up garments for herself so that she was presentable when she appeared in public. No one would ever have guessed how poor we really were from the way we appeared.

Realizing she would have to help financially, Mother rented the vacant lot next door and planted vegetables. When the radishes sprang up, we washed them, tied them in bunches and I sold them from door to door, at *five cents a bunch!* It wasn't easy for a housewife to say "no" to a little barefoot boy with radishes in a basket at five cents a bunch. Needless to say, the radishes sold fast, as did other vegetables as they came into season. And learning to handle money and make change was easy for me!

When I reached the age of five, mother took me to school where I met my teacher, Miss Tweedy. I liked school—enjoyed playing with my classmates and listening to the music Miss Tweedy played on her phonograph with the big wooden horn. Although more than eight decades have passed, the events of that first day are as fresh in my mind as though they were yesterday.

When the circus came to town, Mother helped me arrange a table next to the sidewalk in front of our house where people walked by on their way to the circus. My lemonade sold well to the thirsty walkers on Nebraska's hot days! With each passing day, I became a better salesman, and those early experiences have been valuable to me all my life.

I'll always remember the times my mother sent me to the meat market to buy a ten-cent soup bone. When the butcher looked down at the little barefoot boy holding up a dime, he usually found a sizable bone with meat on it. Mother, of course, knew how to prepare a nutritious meal for the whole family with that bone and her garden vegetables.

One of my many after-school chores was to take a little pail to a dairy at the edge of town each evening and buy a quart of milk. From time to time, there were days when we didn't have the price of milk—a nickel! On those days, we simply went without. I recall how I craved milk.

However, in a family of four, there was only a little more than a tablespoonful of milk for each of us for breakfast. Imagine, if you can, eating oatmeal with only a tablespoon of milk! For me, the so-called "good old days" left much to be desired.

Me at age 10 with my half-brother, Virgil, at age five.

At times, Mother would buy a huge "old rooster" for 50 cents. After boiling the rooster until it was tender, she would add vegetables. Then she would line a large pan with dough, place the chicken and vegetables in the dough-lined pan, cover the top with another layer of dough and bake it. These huge "chicken pies" made excellent Sunday dinners for the whole family—with left-overs for Monday.

Thanks to the exceptional ability and practical intelligence of my mother, we always managed to get by. Working with Mother during those very challenging times proved to be an invaluable experience for me. Finding a way to pay the monthly $10 house rent provided plenty of mental gymnastics in economics, resourcefulness and money management.

At age 10, I delivered the *Fremont Tribune* newspaper for one dollar a week. I learned another one of my "resourceful" lessons at about that age when Gumpert Department Store burned. The grocery department was in the basement of the building and was saved by the water the firemen rained down from above. After the charred embers of the upper floor were removed, piles of canned goods were exposed—not damaged by fire, but without labels! I was told that I could help myself to the cans. With my little red wagon, I hauled load after load to our basement. Then when winter came, we had an abundance of canned food. Of course, we were never sure what the content of each can might be—sauerkraut, pineapple slices, hominy, delicious peaches...it was a guessing game we enjoyed playing! But the contents of the cans always gave us a needed supplement to our diet.

At 11, I bought a second-hand chicken incubator, placed eggs inside and made sure the temperature during the next three weeks was proper. As the chickens hatched, I made a warm place for them and fed them with great care and joy. Then, when the chickens reached the two-pound size, I sold them as "fryers" and made a modest profit. But not enough profit to persuade me to go into the poultry business, I might add!

I also learned to visit the slaughter house, and when I "hung around," the butcher would often give me a cow's liver or heart. This, of course, made a meal for the whole family.

Before the electric refrigerator, we, like our neighbors, depended on the local iceman to deliver ice to our home. He would stop his wagon, open our unlocked kitchen door and deposit a cake of ice in our "icebox." On Saturday, he was paid ten cents for each chunk he delivered during the week. We had to be sure to empty the drip-pan each evening, or else the kitchen would get flooded. As the iceman drove away, all the neighborhood kids would follow until we were given a piece of ice to suck on. This was a luxury we all enjoyed, especially during the hot summer months...and a delight the "electric refrigeration generation" has missed.

In order to stimulate their sales of baking flour, the Pillsbury Flour Company offered a $50 prize to the person who could book the most orders for 50-pound sacks of flour. Well, the $50 prize money sounded very big to my mother, so all that summer, in the 100-degree Nebraska heat, she went door-to-door soliciting orders.

Another lady was equally determined to win the prize money, but in the end, my mother won and was on "cloud nine!" I remember very vividly how she bought herself a tweed suit, along with other things she had her heart set on.

As I've indicated, Mother was unusually resourceful. Although 10-inch-long loaves of bread were only a nickel and the longer loaves only a dime, Mother always baked our bread— and what bread it was! Sometimes she would make cinnamon and raisin rolls from the left-over dough. My mouth still waters when I think of how good they were!

I remember that one of the most exciting events to hit Fremont, Nebraska, in those days, eagerly looked forward to by the town's ladies, was the opening of the new Woolworth 5 & 10¢ Store. As a super promotion for the event, the store advertised that they would sell granite dishpans for 10 cents. Well, talk about crowds! Some people waited for hours to be first in line at the door. Finally, when the store doors opened, the place was mobbed. Outside on the street, one could see the lucky ladies who managed to get a dishpan for 10 cents, proudly carrying it home. Mother was among those who were successful.

When a locomotive jumped the track near where we lived, I brought home the spilled coal in my little red wagon. Naturally, Mother was delighted to have enough coal for cooking to last her for several days.

Among the various things I sold door-to-door was a line of cake flavors—vanilla, lemon and so on—at 25 cents a bottle. Some of my Baptist customers were shocked when they read the printed label: "12 percent alcohol!" On the other hand, my "wino" customer didn't object at all, because he drank it for that reason. Still, some customers wouldn't buy the flavors because of the alcohol content.

To please them, I bought a gross of identical empty bottles, filled them two-thirds full with simple syrup, then filled the upper third with soda fountain vanilla, lemon and other flavors. I dipped the cork in paraffin, capped and shook the contents, and the result was flavors without alcohol—and my profit was slightly greater. The important thing was that my Baptist customers were ecstatic because they could flavor their cakes without alcohol. I have learned in life to give the customers what they want whenever possible.

CHAPTER TWO

My stepfather rarely had a kind word for me, so our relationship was always strained. If I didn't move fast enough to suit him when he ordered me to bring in water, he would slap me on one ear—and if I started to fall, he would slap me on the other. Why I'm not deaf today is a mystery to me. However, I am grateful to my stepfather, because the bad example he set convinced me that "booze" wasn't for me.

Like most boys, I used to daydream about what I would be when I grew up. The dream I enjoyed most was that of owning a farm where everything was white: a white house, white fences, white chickens, white dog, white cows, white horses and white fantail pigeons on the roof. That's one dream I have yet to realize.

Each spring the Platte River flooded our area, and when the water eventually receded, it left ponds with little fish in them. My friends and I loved to explore the remaining ponds. There were sometimes bullhead fish six inches long, with razor-sharp prongs on each side of their jaws that stuck out an inch. On one occasion, I was so excited about having retrieved several bullheads that I was dancing around on my bare feet and inadvertently stepped on one of the fish. A prong imbedded itself in the sole of my bare foot, and not having the will power to yank it out, I crawled the two miles home on my hands and knees—with the bullhead dangling from my foot! On arriving, a neighbor yanked it out, put a little iodine on the gash and added a band-aid.

Our little town was like many others in the mid-America of those days. The bronze fountain on the main corner had a sizable bowl with running water on the street side where horses could drink. On the sidewalk side, there was a continuously running small stream with two brass cups on chains so that people could help themselves. It never occurred to people in those days that they might catch something!

The local dentist displayed a glass cylinder of extracted teeth at the entrance to his street office, with a little sign that read, "Extractions 50¢." Unfortunately, in those days I didn't know that by removing two of my lower crowded teeth, the remaining ones would have grown straight. I have always regretted that I didn't take advantage of that 50-cent special.

From time to time, my maternal grandmother, Mary, would prepare dinner for the entire family of more than a dozen members. One Christmas she had gone all out, with everything from turkey with cranberries to black-walnut cake with chocolate frosting. We all commented how good the food was and how we enjoyed the dinner. Her comment was, "Well, I guess you should. I spent most of five dollars for the makings!"

My mother and her sister, Millie, married brothers—my father, Fred, and my uncle John—which made their children, Marion and Roy, and myself double cousins. My Aunt Millie was like a second mother to me, and her son, Marion, being about my age, became my very close friend. I was often invited to their home in the country. In fact, I spent several summer vacations there, and when I was asked to stay one whole winter and attend the same school as my cousin, I was delighted. The school was in a "one-general-store town" called Fontenelle, three miles from my aunt's farm. My cousin and I enjoyed the three-mile hike to school except in winter when the snow was so deep we could only find our way by following the exposed tops of the fence posts. During cold weather, our lunches had to be thawed out behind the school stove because the boiled eggs and sandwiches would freeze solid.

During the fall months, the changing colors of the foliage made the canyons and countryside with their old oaks very beautiful. I had an eye for beauty—and also for profit. I noticed holes in the side of an embankment. Well, I decided it must be some fur-bearing animal's home, and if I caught and skinned the animal, I could sell the hide. So, I set a trap in the hole opening, and the next day I had caught myself a black and white skunk! I continued on to school, but on my arrival I was promptly sent home because of the odor the skunk had sprayed on me. Not to be dissuaded, on the way back home, I killed the skunk, brought it with me and skinned it and tacked its hide on a shed to dry. Then, I buried all my clothes in the ground and scrubbed myself with strong soap. The next day, I was able to return to school. And when I delivered my skunk pelt to a furrier, I received two dollars for it. Later, I caught muskrats along the shore of the lake, and their skins helped keep me in pocket money.

The school I attended was a two-room structure. In one room, where my cousin and I sat, our teacher taught the first through the fourth grades. In the other room, the fifth through the eighth grades were taught. My teacher, Miss Tenbrink, took a personal interest in me. I wasn't as robust as most of the boys in my class. At that time in Nebraska, a boy's prospects were gaged by his brawn. If a boy couldn't shuck corn or handle bales of hay, his future wasn't considered promising. Miss Tenbrink told me, "Don't be discouraged, George. There are jobs that don't require brawn. For example, the telegraph operators in every railroad station have good-paying, inside jobs."

To encourage me, she even bought me a $2.50 Morse code keyboard and an instruction book from her $60 a month salary. I learned the Morse code and how to send messages, but I never got one of those good-paying jobs with a railroad! Years later when Miss Tenbrink retired on her pathetic school pension, I was in a financial position to supplement her modest income each month for 15 years.

Life with my cousin on my aunt and uncle's farm was a complete change for me. Five o'clock was "get-up time," and after each of us had milked two cows, we then ran the milk through a separator to extract the cream that my uncle delivered to the creamery. The "skimmed" milk, we fed to the pigs. Today, that "worthless" nonfat milk sells for almost the same as whole milk.

Each Saturday, Uncle John hitched the mules to the spring wagon for the trip to the town of Nickerson, 15 miles away. He would drop off the cream at the creamery, and Aunt Millie would bring her week's accumulation of eggs, together with large crocks of butter that she had churned, to turn in at the grocery store for credit on the family grocery bill. She usually managed to have enough credit to pay for the groceries. The trip to Nickerson gave her a chance to greet old friends and catch up on the latest gossip: "Yes, the Browns are expecting; the Smiths are selling their prize bull; the Jones' prize sow won a blue ribbon"—and other exciting news. My uncle also enjoyed seeing and greeting old friends and exchanging experiences.

From time to time, a "box social" was held in the lodge hall over the grocery store, and on those occasions, a fiddler and pianist entertained while people played games until auction time. When the auction began, one by one the young single women proudly presented their fancy boxes filled with tasty goodies. The "young bucks" would bid on the boxes, competing with one another in the hope of sharing the contents with a popular young lady.

On other occasions, the older ladies competed by making preserves, mincemeat pies and cakes. Other contests involved the sewing of fancy, hand-made bedspreads and quilts made from hundreds of small pieces of material. Aunt Millie had such a quilt that she had made, with a hemstitched outline of my hand when I was two years old. I've often wondered what became of that quilt.

Each morning and evening my aunt washed the many parts of the cream separator and, to prevent bacteria, scalded each part. This was done by heating kettles of water on her corn-cob-burning cook stove, the same stove she used to prepare meals for her family of big eaters. She somehow also found time to churn and make butter and can vegetables and all kinds of fruits in season. Of course, she did the family wash by hand on a washboard, too, along with washing diapers and sanitary napkins. All this was just naturally expected as women's work! Our modern conveniences were still a hidden dream, undiscovered.

When Uncle John butchered the 200-pound hogs, my aunt took on the job of cutting up the parts, making sausage and putting pieces into barrels of salt brine. In the absence of modern refrigeration systems, slabs of bacon and other parts of the pork could only be preserved in salt brine or by smoking it over special wood.

When thrashing time came, Aunt Millie would prepare huge meals for a dozen hungry workers. In winter, when the washing would freeze on the line, she would have to bring it in and hang it around the heater to thaw. In spite of this heavy workload, my little 98-pound aunt enjoyed a healthy life to the age of 90. When my uncle died, she lived alone on the farm. Later, I had a television set delivered to her, and she was so excited that she stayed up nights to watch it. It brought the whole world into her home during the long, cold winters when storms and deep snow made it difficult to go out. Farm life in those days was hard for both men and women; however, somehow they managed—and were none the worse for it.

Standing in the back is me at age 11 with my hand on the shoulder of my half-brother, Oliver, my mother holding my half-brother Virgil at age 2, and on her left is my full-brother, Harold, standing.

CHAPTER THREE

When I was 13 years old, I was able to get a job at Yager Nursery during summer vacation. I would set my alarm for five, make my breakfast, pack my own lunch and walk three miles to meet the wagon at the nursery shed. The wagon would take about 20 of us boys to the place where the nursery was growing seedlings. Each boy was assigned a row, and we had to crawl along on our hands and knees, pulling the weeds from between the little trees. At 10 o'clock a jug of water was passed around, and at noon we stopped for lunch. By one o'clock, we were back at work until seven in the evening, when we completed a 12-hour shift—at 5 cents an hour, 60 cents a day, $3.60 for a six-day week. The money I earned in this way enabled me to send to Sears Roebuck for my winter school clothes and shoes, and also for blankets for the bed that I shared with my brothers.

By this time, my mother had borne two other sons, Oliver and Virgil, by my stepfather, John Tipton. We boys were about three years apart.

Tipton was a little more humane toward his own sons than he was toward me and my full brother, Harold. Being the eldest, I was the one expected to bring in the water, get fuel and peddle vegetables. Although I didn't appreciate it at the time, I later realized that it gave me experience that has helped me all my life.

One day while working for the nursery, I noticed a huge pile of cottonwood saplings in a shed. I asked if there was a market for them. They told me that, indeed, there was a market for the little trees—for use as windbreaks. I asked how much the nursery could afford to pay for more of the saplings. "Well, we have another order for 50,000 and would pay a dollar a thousand for them," they said. Knowing how numerous the cottonwood seedlings were along the Platte River near my uncle's farm, I felt confident my cousin and I could easily supply 50,000 saplings for the nursery. So, I offered to deliver the saplings at the price of a dollar per thousand—and even signed a contract.

When my cousin, Marion, and I explored the river bed, we had no difficulty in pulling up the required 50,000 saplings. We tied them in bundles of 500 and "sweet-talked" Uncle John into making the delivery to the nursery, where we were given a check for $50. We split the money, and although we both had large blisters on our hands from pulling up the saplings, we felt very rich.

One winter when the lake was frozen over, I was told that if we made a hole in the ice, the fish would come up for air. So, Marion and I cut a hole—and sure enough, the fish came to the hole by the hundreds. We bailed them out until we had a pile several feet high. Then with more "sweet talk," we persuaded Uncle John to haul the fish to Fremont for us. There, we made the rounds of the meat markets and restaurants—but no sale!

Finally, the owner of a fish market told us that the fish we caught were "carp," and that carp were very popular with certain ethnic groups. He suggested that we stand in front of the synagogue with a sign, and the passersby would become our prospects. We acted quickly. We found our new territory and made a sign: "For Sale, Fresh Carp, Just Caught." We held up our sign and smiled confidently at everyone who walked toward us. In no time at all, every fish was sold—neatly wrapped in newspaper sheets, which was the "customized wrapper" in those days. Well, our fish experience taught us perseverance...to never give up or lose hope!

Back home when school was in session, I couldn't hold a full-time job, but I needed to earn money. I had learned in school how to print letters by hand, and that ability suggested an idea. I decided to cut out pictures of attractive fashion models from magazines, paste the cutouts on cardboard, then add a suitable message. I would show a poster to a tailor's shop, for example, with a message like "Fine Tailoring and Alterations," or "Smith's Tailor Shop" or some other message to suit the owner. Some of the posters featured pictures of ladies, and that appealed to tailors who catered to that trade. I was sometimes able to sell two or three posters an evening for two dollars each, and that kept the wolf from the door. At grammar school graduation time, the school paid me 50 cents each to fill in the students' names on the diplomas, in Old English typestyle.

By now, our family had moved to Omaha, Nebraska, where my stepfather got a job on the police force and at last was making steady wages. He and Mother rented a two bedroom flat, with running water, gas lights and indoor plumbing. What luxury! No more kerosene lamp shades to clean or pails of water to fetch from an outside pump. And indoor plumbing was, of course, the ultimate in luxury...especially in cold weather!

As I approached my sixteenth birthday, my stepfather informed me that it was time for me to "paddle my own canoe," as he put it. So, I packed all my worldly possessions in a shoe box, took a streetcar to the edge of town where the Lincoln highway passed and started thumbing my way west...to California, where oranges—like the one my teacher had given me for Christmas when I was 11—grew on trees! That gift of one piece of fruit had persuaded me that I should one day live where it had come from.

The idea of anyone traveling any great distance by hitchhiking was unknown at that time. Cars didn't travel at such high speeds then, and it was considered unfriendly to pass someone who was walking without offering him a lift. So, I had rides in no time at all. Although some were only for a short distance, by the end of the first day, the rides had taken me more than a hundred miles. I then found a YMCA where I could have a shower and sleep on a cot for 50 cents. Not having much money, I made a five-cent Hershey bar satisfy my noon appetite. But for dinner I would order a ten-cent bowl of bean soup, put in lots of catsup and then fill the bowl with crackers. So, I had dinner for a dime.

Some of the people I rode with would take me to lunch, and that was always welcome. Getting a ride was so easy that I soon became "choosey." When a truck or load of freight approached me, I would walk toward them, to discourage them from stopping. The same with old model cars! I preferred to wait for a shiny deluxe car, like a late model Jackrabbit, a bright Studebaker, a Packard or Pierce Arrow. I learned that the larger cars were usually going farther and were not driven by people who were merely returning home from shopping!

In spite of being careful, my funds were running low. Near Denver, I noticed a sign on a fence that read, "Boy wanted to thin peach blossoms." Well, that sounded like nice work, so I applied for the job. The farmer explained that he wanted a light-weight boy to climb the trees and thin the blossoms to one every six inches, so that when the fruit developed it wouldn't be so heavy that it broke the limbs. The job paid a dollar a day, with board and room, for a 12-hour day. I took it, and at the end of seven days I was paid seven silver dollars. Since that time I have had some profitable deals, but never have I felt as rich as I did with those seven big silver dollars in my pocket!

I resumed my journey to California and soon had the good fortune of being picked up by a couple with a son about my age in a brand new Pierce Arrow. Their son had been bored and lonely in the back seat by himself, so his parents were glad to have company for him. The family invited me to come with them to Yellowstone National Park. I liked the idea but wondered how I would manage at night. There were no 50-cent YMCAs in Yellowstone, I felt sure. To give me peace of mind, they suggested I sleep on the big back seat of the car. "With the side curtains up, it will be cozy," they said.

When we arrived in Yellowstone, we saw Old Faithful perform and enjoyed the scenery and wildlife. That first night, I put up the side curtains and had just gotten myself comfortable when a loud noise made me jump up. It sounded as though the rear of the car was being ripped off. The park bears had gotten a whiff of the lunch meat in the trunk of the car and were tearing it apart to get the meat. I was very frightened, because I thought they might want *me* for the second course! But having gotten the meat, they lumbered off—and I got a good night's sleep, with no further disturbances.

The park was all I hoped it would be, with lots of bears, elk and buffalo. But by the third day, I was beginning to feel quite hungry, living on nothing but a Hershey-bar diet. That's when I made the acquaintance of a young park ranger. As we talked, he said he had a cabin nearby where he lived with his wife. He talked about how he loved to catch trout, and I agreed that it must be great sport. Before we parted, he invited me to join him for a trout dinner at his cabin. Well, he didn't have to coax me—at the agreed hour, I was there! Just as I arrived at his cabin, he came walking up with a string of rainbow trout. In no time, he had a campfire going, had cleaned the trout and put them in a big pan over the hot coals. Since that time, I have been privileged to enjoy trout prepared by the top chefs of big New York hotels and by the master chefs on cross-Atlantic liners, but never have I experienced trout with the aroma or scrumptious taste of the trout prepared by that park ranger over his campfire so long ago!

After three memorable days in the park, my friends were ready to travel on. Their plan was to head directly toward San Francisco. However, I was set on going straight to Los Angeles by way of Salt Lake, so after my thanks and good-byes, we parted.

When I arrived in Salt Lake City, I was impressed by the huge Mormon Temple and the Tabernacle where I enjoyed the choir singing. Then I headed for the famous Great Salt Lake where I had a swim and satisfied myself that I couldn't sink!

Arizona came next, with its giant cacti, some of which were in bloom and very beautiful. The roads got progressively worse, then we hit the "corduroy highway." It was made of logs laid side by side—bumpy, to be sure, but better than the dust filled chuckholes.

Finally, I crossed the state line into California, and I still had $2.30 in my pocket! It can't be said that I arrived broke! What a joy it was when I began to see palms and orange trees at last! In those days, there was no smog—the air was clean and refreshing. Having never seen a body of water that I couldn't look across, I was anxious to see the Pacific Ocean. I was told that the "Red Car," an electric street-car line, would take me to Long Beach. So, I made the trip to Long Beach—and sure enough, I couldn't see across the Pacific Ocean! To verify that it was salty, I tasted it and, sure enough again, it was. Then I put on a rented bathing suit and had an enjoyable swim.

At the bathhouse, I met a young man about my age, and when I mentioned that I needed to look for a job, he said he had just heard that the swanky Virginia Hotel was looking for an elevator operator. I told him I had never operated an elevator, and he said, "Don't tell them that, or you'll never get the job. It's simple," he continued, "just put the lever on the number of the floor."

Well, I applied for the job, and when they asked me if I had experience, I assured them I had. So they put me in a uniform and asked me to take a dowager to the fourth floor. Not wishing to appear inexperienced, I swung the lever to the figure four with great authority—but in my desire to impress the lady with my expertise, I evidently went past four. The elevator hit the ceiling so hard that my passenger fell on the elevator floor and began screaming for help. When I finally managed to get down to her floor, staff members attracted by her screams helped her up and out. I never heard what she reported about me, but it couldn't have been too favorable. Upon reaching the ground floor, the manager greeted me with, "You're fired!" The lesson I learned from that experience was that bluffing about know-how entailed risks!

In 1917, America became involved in World War I, and many young men were enlisting in the armed forces. I decided to join, too, but when the recruiter saw the "down" on my face, he asked how old I was. "Sixteen," I replied.

"Well, you come back in a year," said the recruiter.

"So, I must wait at least a year before they want me in the service," I thought. "The question is, what shall I do for a whole year?" I gave the matter serious consideration and decided that it would be a good time to see more of the United States.

CHAPTER FOUR

I knew I loved California, but I'd never seen Florida. "Perhaps, I'd like it even better," I thought. "Maybe I should set out for Florida." But it was June, the perfect time to visit Oregon and Washington, and since hitchhiking was so easy, I decided to travel north, instead.

My former hitchhiking experiences had taught me to travel light, with never more than a paper bag or shoe box that could pass for a lunch box. I wore tennis shoes that I kept snow white by applying whitener as often as needed. I never walked much, so it was easy to keep them clean. At night, I washed my knit shirt that didn't require ironing, and somehow I managed to always look like a clean-cut school boy deserving a ride. Never did I ever even consider bumming my way on a night train! That wasn't for me. It was too dangerous and dirty, and I'd found a much more pleasant way to get from place to place—in the daylight. With a shower and a bed to sleep in at the local YMCAs, the so-called hardships of travel never bothered me.

I stopped two days in San Francisco, and from the lobby writing room in the St. Francis Hotel, I sent my mother a long letter on their stationery. I loved the city's little cable cars, Fisherman's Wharf and Golden Gate Park. But I had to press on.

I traveled north to beautiful Portland and then Seattle, where I was delighted to see the old "gingerbread" homes of the lumber tycoons. As I traveled on toward Canada, I stopped in Washington at a town near the northwest corner of the United States called Bellingham. The big industry there was salmon fishing and canning.

As I explored the docks, I happened to meet a sea captain who answered questions for me concerning the fishing industry. As we got better acquainted, he pointed out his boat that would be going out to bring in tons of salmon that same night. Seeing how interested I was, he asked if I'd like to go along. "Indeed, I would," I answered. So later, I went aboard his boat, and he made me welcome. By midnight, we had reached the place where his nets were set. The boat's cranes started lifting the nets, and tons of wiggling salmon were dumped on the deck. Then the fish were shoveled into ice bunkers. Seeing this operation was fascinating to me, and I thanked the captain for the experience and for the dinner in the galley. His cook had prepared a delicious fresh salmon that I enjoyed immensely.

On returning from my sailing adventure, I traveled on to Vancouver Island, British Columbia. I enjoyed the ripe blackberries that grew along the highway. The town of Victoria, which is the capital of the province, was charming, and when I learned of its famous Butchart Gardens, I went to see this man-made canyon created by the removal of material to make cement. I was told that the wife of the owner felt duty-bound to overcome the gaping, unsightly hole in the ground. She employed a landscaper, planted acres of gardens and created a showplace where people come by the thousands to enjoy the natural beauty.

As a teenage boy from Nebraska, it seemed strange being in a foreign country. It was, of course, the first time I'd ever been across the U.S. border. The Canadians were so polite and friendly, and I loved their beautiful country. However, their newspapers, like ours, were full of stories of the war in Europe.

Upon returning to the state of Washington, I traveled east to Spokane and then on to Idaho, Wyoming and North Dakota. Each day, I would cover at least a hundred miles and often more. I passed through St. Paul, Minnesota, and then journeyed on to Milwaukee, Wisconsin, where I visited the huge Schlitz Brewery and saw how beer was made. From there, I made my way to the big city of Chicago, Illinois, where I spent a day in the fabulous Field Museum and then paid a visit to the Swift Company slaughter house and stockyards. There, I saw cattle and hogs being butchered and processed on a gigantic scale. Nothing was allowed to be wasted, not even the blood from the animals. As they cut the animals' throats, the blood was trapped in a gutter and by some process reduced to a dried powder and sold for fertilizer. I was interested, too, in my visit to the Marshall Field department store, by far the largest of any I had ever seen.

Before continuing east, I decided to drop down to Omaha and visit my mother. I had kept in touch by sending her scenic postcards all along the way and by writing home on stationery from the writing rooms of the big hotels. I never told her I was a guest in the hotels, nor did I say I wasn't. In fact, I never explained how I financed my travels and got from place to place. Mother had learned to expect the unusual from me and just assumed that I had the ability to earn money and pay my own way. She and my brothers were happy to see me, but in order not to crowd them in their two bedroom flat, I took a room at the local YMCA for the several days of my stay.

From Omaha, I traveled to Detroit, where I visited the Ford Motor Company factory and saw Fords being built. Then it was on through the great corn belt of our country—through Illinois, Indiana, Ohio and into New York State. I was enormously impressed by the spectacular view of Niagara Falls (often known as "honeymooners paradise") with its tremendous volume of water and the beauty of ever so many rainbows over the crashing waters. I put on rain-gear and actually went under the falls. Interestingly, Niagara Falls is a city within the metropolitan area of Buffalo, the second largest city in the state of New York. A bridge, known as Peace Bridge, connects Niagara Falls to Fort Erie, Ontario, Canada. The Peace Bridge was opened in 1927 to commemorate 100 years of peace between the United States and Canada.

I turned north to see New England, crossing Vermont with its excavations to quarry marble. The sawing of the marble into huge blocks and then into slabs was very interesting to me. Vermont also is the source of much of our maple syrup.

I went as far as the state of Maine, with its rugged coastline and fishing industry, then returned south to Boston, Massachusetts, where the Christian Science Mother Church and many tourist attractions are located. When I had seen New England and had my fill of lobster, I traveled on down the eastern seaboard.

Fall was coming, and the leaves were beginning to turn from green to gold, amber and crimson. I arrived in New York City, which is, of course, "where the action is." What a city! I loved the Metropolitan Museum, with its wealth of artifacts and fine paintings. The Egyptian exhibits were especially fantastic for me. Central Park, in the heart of the city, impressed me, and I very much enjoyed the many theaters. Following my established pattern, I wrote a letter to my mother from the writing room of the world famous Waldorf Astoria Hotel. "Every newspaper is filled with the news of the War," I told her.

I crossed the state of Delaware on my way to our nation's capital, Washington, D.C. The beauty of the Capitol Building and the fine art galleries were inspiring, and the Smithsonian Museum was impressive. But I also remember that men in uniform were everywhere. "I can't wait to be accepted into the military," I thought at the time.

By now, I had become sufficiently expert at painting signs on glass with either paint or gold leaf that I was able to solicit work hand-lettering messages on shop windows. This gave me more pocket money. I still slept in YMCAs at 50 cents a night and was able to keep going on surprisingly little money. On the entire trip around the country, I managed to never be sick or out of money even one day.

As I continued south from the capital, I found that I enjoyed the city of Atlanta very much, with its Peachtree main street. Even though I worked at acquiring the Georgians' Southern accent, I was never good at it; everyone knew immediately that I was a "Yankee." But they were courteous and kind to me, so I became very fond of the South.

I was anxious to get to Florida, because I knew that it, like California, had orange and palm trees. "Who knows?" I thought. "I might like Florida even better than California!"

Jacksonville was just another commercial town, but St. Augustine was quaint and picturesque. Daytona Beach and Orlando had charming beaches that were popular for auto races because of the solid sand, but I wasn't enamored by the towns. But on arriving in Palm Beach, I was wide-eyed as I saw the luxurious shops, fine clubs and magnificent beach homes! Of course, I never could have guessed that at some future time I would actually be a guest there in Palm Beach at the exclusive Everglades Country Club—that I would be a house guest of Meriweather Post, the breakfast food heiress. As a young man, I couldn't even imagine that I would be there someday at her own private golf course and at her palatial Palm Beach residence...having lunch on her Florentine marble table with inlaid flowers and fruits made of semiprecious stones, including real pearls for dewdrops...being entertained in the elegant beach homes of the affluent. All this came years later!

Traveling on south to Miami Beach, the roads were perfect and the scenery unsurpassed. But the region was humid, and the mosquitoes and insects were terrible! After Miami, I continued even further south on the Causeway—all the way down to Key West. It was very hot and tropical, but I'm glad I went there. I had arrived at the exact opposite location of Bellingham, Washington, which is the northwest corner of the United States—because Key West is in the extreme *southeast* corner. I couldn't see Cuba, but I knew it wasn't far away. On my return, I decided to cross the Everglades by the new highway that had been cut through the lush jungle, with its swamps and abundant wildlife. Alligators would crawl across the road, and drivers had to be careful not to run over them. I thought the variety of birds was spectacular and particularly fascinating to see.

I grew to love the way the people talked— with their soft Southern accents. And their warm hospitality was simply overwhelming. I was invited into several Southern homes and had the real Southern cooking. In fact, I became very fond of hush puppies and fried catfish. On one occasion, I even tasted that Southern delicacy of roasted 'possum.

The swamps were mysterious and fascinating, with heavy moss hanging from nearly every tree branch; but the swamps also were alive with insects that bit unmercifully. Still, I enjoyed seeing all those sights and experiencing what they were like. As I think back, a most interesting sight was to see the hundreds of black people picking cotton by hand; the machine for picking was not yet being used.

The French Quarter in New Orleans was almost like a visit to France, with all the wrought iron balconies and French-speaking natives. Louisiana was even more humid than Florida, but the mosquitoes weren't quite as bad. It was strange to often have the people I passed on the road greet me in French—especially when I stopped to gather pecans! The nuts fell onto the roadside from the trees that grew along the highway. The thin pecan shells are easily cracked by pressing together two nuts in the palm of one's hand.

I remember seeing chain gangs of prisoners in striped suits doing roadwork in that part of the country. The felons were under the supervision of an armed guard, who made sure none of them escaped! All of the rest rooms in the South at that time had four compartments: one each for white women, black women, white men and black men. The blacks had to be careful to "stay in their places," for to be caught in a white area was, indeed, a serious offense.

I found the rich taste of the plump pecan meats delicious, and I was tempted to linger in Louisiana. But the state of Texas was calling me, so I headed west! The cities of Houston and San Antonio were interesting, but neither appealed to me as a place to settle down. The westward roads gradually got worse, often offering only unpaved dirt that developed chuck holes and clouds of dust. For miles, I was forced to reach up and hold onto the supporting top boughs of the vehicle to avoid being hurled from my seat. The ruts would fill with dust, so that a driver couldn't see them until it was too late. Interesting scenery, with large herds of cattle, helped make up for the rough riding to some extent.

When I arrived in New Mexico, I visited Carlsbad Caverns and saw the strange underground caves where thousands of bats lived within the darkness. Across the vast empty spaces, many of the great Southwestern cacti were in bloom and graced the desert with true beauty.

As we approached California, there were miles of those "corduroy roads" I mentioned earlier, highways made by laying logs side by side on the loose desert sands. They were an improvement over the chuckholes, but I was glad when we finally crossed the California state line at Brawley. Soon thereafter, we started seeing date palms and orange, grapefruit and tangerine trees, all growing along the paved roadway under the beautiful, blue California sky. Since there were no fences, I felt obligated to sample the fruit, of course!

California looked better than ever to me after seeing so many other states—yes, even including the "other" orange-growing state, Florida. I was now thoroughly convinced that California was where I wanted to make my permanent home. The state may not be perfect, but it comes the closest, in my opinion. So, I was back in "God's country," and I felt wonderful being in California!

The extensive tour of the United States had been an outstanding educational experience, as well as an interesting and fun-filled time in my life. I couldn't have learned as much if I had spent the time attending one of our great universities. Besides seeing the wonders of our great nation first hand, I also had met thousands of people from every walk of life. Associating with the people with whom I rode, often for several hours, I got to know the variety of different personalities. I was exposed to men from many professions, with widely differing philosophies, ideas and traits—some as different as day and night. For the most part, they were thoughtful, kind and considerate. I learned the art of listening and encouraging men to tell their life story—both the good and the bad—and they often gave me good advice and warned me about "bad" company. All my life I will benefit from what I learned from the people with whom I traveled America.

CHAPTER FIVE

With World War I coming to a close, it appeared that I wouldn't be needed by "Uncle Sam." I could begin to make my life plans. Even though I was only 17 at the time, I was very determined to be in business for myself. Since any business I entered would require capital, I decided to take any kind of job I could find and save my money until I had what it took to start my own business.

Walking down the streets of Los Angeles one day, I saw a sign in Boos Brothers Cafeteria window that read, "Bus Boy Wanted." I reasoned, "Well, I know how to drive a Ford, so I should be able to drive a bus." I applied and was informed that the job had nothing to do with "driving a bus," that it was simply carrying trays of dirty dishes from the dining room to the kitchen. The job paid $13 per week, plus meals, for six 12-hour days.

What I could save and bank was limited. But when I learned that next door they wanted a "soda jerk" to work from 7 p.m. until midnight, and that it paid $12 a week for six nights, I applied and got the job. With both the evening and the daytime jobs, and including my tips, I was able to save $20 a week. Paying $3 a week for a room, however, seemed high to me. So, when I noticed an unused cupola on the top of the rooming house, I asked what it would rent for. "There's no plumbing or electricity on that floor," said the landlady.

I replied, "If I take it as is, manage with the bathroom on the lower floor, wash the windows, put up curtains and install my own furniture, would you rent it to me for $3 a month?"

The landlady thought it over and agreed to let me have the cupola at my price. After I cleaned it, put up curtains and installed an army surplus cot and an orange crate for a chair, I was comfortable—and able to increase my savings to $25 a week. I didn't mind sharing the bath on the lower floor with several others. In fact, I took my showers at the YMCA. And I didn't mind working from seven in the morning until midnight, because I was acquiring capital!

Although my cupola accommodations gave me a nice view and fresh air, I realized it was a firetrap. In case of fire, my chances of getting out alive were not good. To solve this problem, I bought a long surplus rope, tied a knot every three feet, then tied one end securely around the window frame. If an emergency occurred, I could then toss the rope out of the window and let myself down, with my descent slowed by the tied knots. I never had occasion to put the rope to use, but it gave me peace of mind knowing that it was ready should the need arise.

Me at age 19

As the holidays approached, I thought of my mother and three brothers back in Nebraska. They had never seen things like pomegranates, avocados, tangerines, California dates, and big navel oranges. I thought it would be nice to make up a Christmas gift box of assorted California fruits! So, I got a box, lined it with red paper and arranged the fruit in it. I added nuts and tinsel to give it a Christmas appearance.

When the other roomers saw what I was doing, they liked the idea of sending loved ones a gift box of fruit, and they asked if I would make boxes for them. In the days before Christmas, I made a total of 37 boxes for the roomers in my rooming house. "Well," I reasoned, "if there is a demand for 37 gift boxes in this one rooming house, a store featuring such gifts should do well." And...by the next fall, I had accumulated more than $1,000 in my bank account for an investment.

When the supervisor where I worked learned of my plan to quit and start my own business, he called me into his office. He told me they were pleased with my services and planned to promote me and give me a pay raise if I stayed with them. "With us," he continued, "you will have security and can work your way up in our organization. To start your own business is very risky. Most new businesses fail and wind up in bankruptcy. With us you'll have security and work into a prestigious position. Think it over, and hopefully you'll decide to stay with us at a higher salary."

It was very tempting. But my mind was made up—I wanted to be in business for myself. So, I thanked him for his interest and resigned to be free to start my own business.

Universal Studios, where many films were made in those days, was very close to Los Angeles. So, I decided to pay it a visit. The bus dropped me off at the studio entrance, and not seeing a "keep out" sign, I ventured in and toured the lot. Several groups of actors were in the process of making motion pictures, with directors shouting instructions via megaphones. I enjoyed watching the comic stunts, especially when pies were thrown in the actor's face. Just as I was ready to leave, someone asked me if I'd like to participate in a film involving a classroom scene that was being shot that afternoon. When I said "yes," the makeup man made me ready, and I joined a group of young "ham" actors.

The director asked that we start "acting" and see how much trouble we could make for the "teacher." And, indeed, we went into "action!" In no time at all, the classroom was in shambles, but that's what the director said he wanted! At the end of the scene, I was paid two dollars, and I caught the bus back to Los Angeles. After that experience, I casually mentioned in my next letter home that I had just returned from Universal Studios where I had acted in the schoolroom scene of a motion picture—and that I had been paid *in dollars* for my role as an actor in the film!

During this time, it was not the style to have hair below the neckline, down on the back of the neck, so I had to get regular haircuts. The going price of haircuts, at 50 cents, seemed high to me. So, I would go to a "barber college," where the price was only 25 cents.

If I was lucky enough to get a barber student who had cut several heads of hair before mine, I could usually avoid the "stair step" look— because by that time, he had gained a little expertise in hair cutting. I will never forget, however, the time I drew a new student, and I was his first "patient" (client). I not only went home with a "stair step" hairdo, but I was sporting two Band-Aids where he had nicked me!

In the fall, I rented a store on Hill Street near the Clark Hotel. It cost me $500 for the month before Christmas. From raw lumber, I built shelves and tables. I covered the wood with paper, then arranged a display of gift boxes and baskets of assorted fruits and nuts. I arose at four in the morning, went to the wholesale fruit market and bought my supplies for the orders. I opened for business at nine in the morning and closed at seven in the evening. Then at night, in the basement of my rooming house, I packed the orders I had taken during the day and they were ready for shipping early the next morning. Even though it was a one-man operation during that first year, it convinced me that the gift pack business had a potential. So, I registered the name "Mission Pak" and planned to open more stores the following holiday season. Of course, with more than one store, I would have to hire several helpers.

All this planning was exciting, because I had found a business that I liked very much—that didn't require a big investment. It did, however, require *some* capital, mainly for store rental—money that had to be paid in advance. Therefore, in the beginning, I was limited as to how many stores I could rent.

Initially, there was also the problem of persuading landlords to rent their stores for a short period of time to an 18-year-old boy—who looked 17! It took all the sales persuasion at my command to convince each landlord that it was good business for him to rent on a temporary basis for a fraction of the usual rental...to a youngster he didn't know.

It was only after several years—and the ability to provide a financial statement proving that I had a profitable business—that the banks would even consider making me a loan. Being in a business where I had to pay, in advance, for rent and merchandise and then wait until December 10th for the sales receipts was very much a handicap. When I finally established bank credit and, of course, didn't need it, the banks were eager to give me loans.

There was something novel and different about my Mission Pak business. The business grew, and I opened more stores each year. In time, I was operating as many as 100 stores from

San Diego to San Francisco and Sacramento, with more than 1,000 employees, counting those in the packing plant and in the office in Los Angeles.

An early Mission Pak store

As the business grew, my own work load increased greatly. Each year, more stores had to be leased, made ready, stocked and operated for the season—then torn down. When the season was over and the business finally came to a close, however, I was free to travel...and this I did.

CHAPTER SIX

In 1925, I booked passage on the Cunard steamship *California* for a first-class, round-the-world cruise. The cost was $600. Bear in mind, though, that this was the day of the two-cent postage stamp. A loaf of bread was 10 cents; today the same loaf will cost more than a dollar. So, to get a fair comparison of the cost of the cruise in today's money, you must multiply by at least 10! I enjoyed every minute of the cruise, and although my inside cabin was not air-conditioned, I was too excited by the trip to mind. On warm nights I just slept on deck, out in the open. It was a great adventure for a lad of 24!

Our first stop on the cruise after leaving Long Beach Harbor was Hawaii, then we sailed on to fascinating Japan. The earthquake of 1923, two years earlier, had destroyed most of Yokohama and a good part of Tokyo. One exception was Tokyo's Imperial Hotel, designed by Frank Lloyd Wright. It had little damage because of Wright's ingenious engineering and design. I liked my room at the Imperial, although the only heat was a jardiniere of charcoal kept burning by the staff day and night.

I lost no time finding a ricksha puller who spoke English, so that I could see what remained of Tokyo. As we passed through Yokohama, I was curious about the long row of new two-story houses near the harbor. I learned that the structures were among the first things built after the quake. At that time, prostitution was a government monopoly and was especially profitable near the harbor where ship hands, fresh from a long sea voyage, were eager for diversion. The street side of the new buildings was open, and on the walls inside were large photos of attractive Japanese girls. All a prospective client had to do was point to the picture that appealed to him, and the "madam" would show him upstairs to that particular young lady. The government-regulated price for girls' "services" was set at two dollars. I learned later that the girls were recruited from families that needed money, and it was considered an honor for a young woman to volunteer to help her parents financially. At the end of five years or so, the girls had fulfilled their contract, and they were returned home. Being experts at pleasing men, these girls were sought after by young farmers who were looking for wives.

I wanted to see the colossal bronze statue of the Great Buddha at Kamakura, so my ricksha puller took me there. Its tremendous size was simply awesome, and so were the thousands upon thousands of pilgrims who flocked to see it. The sight was overwhelming.

At that time, the Japanese believed their Emperor had actually descended from heaven. He had ridden down on a great white horse, they said, and if I doubted it, they would show me the horse! I said, "Yes, I'd like to see his horse!" And sure enough, they showed me an immaculately groomed, white horse in a fancy stall!

I traveled by automobile along a winding road that followed the old cryptomeria trees, set out by pilgrims, to the sacred grounds of Nikko. There were two bridges at the entry, but I was told to take the one on the right; the other was reserved for spirits only. The Nikko shrine was beautiful beyond belief, with polished lacquered floors—and we had to remove our shoes before entering.

We were too early for the cherry blossoms, but the rock gardens and the Mikado's residence on an island in the center of Tokyo were very attractive. From there, I was taken to a mountain resort hotel in Mijanoshita, near Hakone, where all the floors and steps were covered with white cloth, changed daily.

The currency exchange rate at that time was so favorable that I stocked up on custom-made silk shirts, with handmade button holes, for $2.50 each! I had tailored suits for the tropics made overnight at a cost of $5.00 each. At the time of our departure, my English-speaking guide presented me with a 12-inch ivory man and monkey—and after almost 70 years, I still have the artifact in my home.

I felt like a giant as I walked down the streets of Tokyo, because I could look over the heads of the average Japanese. This is no longer true today; now, the children sit on chairs in school instead of folding their legs under them, which cut off circulation and dwarfed their growth. Also, they now eat a more balanced diet and take vitamins.

Before leaving Japan, I visited an embroidery factory where hundreds of boys from 10 years of age and up were doing exquisite hand embroidery work. I was told that by their early teens, the boys' eyes couldn't take the exacting labor. I also wanted to visit the place where they grew pearls, but time didn't permit.

We steamed on to Hong Kong where I took the funicular, an escalator-tram device, to the top of a mountain for a magnificent view of the bay. The shops were filled with magnificent artifacts, including finely carved jade and ivory. The jewelry shops had bushels of pearls and diamonds heaped in their show windows and were very reasonably priced at that time.

After Hong Kong, we cruised to Canton, China, then on to Ceylon. Each evening the ship's orchestra would play dance music on deck. Without air conditioning, it was too warm inside, so they sprinkled cornmeal on deck and we danced in the open. It was delightful—and being single at that time, I could "pick and choose" my dancing partners.

Batavia Java, under Dutch control, was a delightful place—so clean and well organized. Then I journeyed on to Calcutta, with its hoards of humanity. My train accommodations to Benares consisted of a boxcar with benches around the inside perimeter, and in the center of the car was a 300-pound cake of ice. The windows were kept shut to keep out the heat, and since there were only men in the car, we stripped down to our shorts and hugged the ice to keep cool. At each stop, we looked out of the windows and could see thousands of hungry people. The streams were full of fish, but their Hindu religion told them, "Don't kill any living thing." So, the hungry people just milled around in the heat. The sacred bulls would wander through the streets and eat vegetables and fruit from the open air stands, but the merchants dared not drive them away.

The sacred city of Benares was very intriguing—with people bathing in the river, drinking the same water, and burning their dead on funeral pyres along the banks. If a family's means permitted, enough sandalwood was used to burn the relative's body completely. But if means were limited, the body was sometimes only partially burned before throwing the remains into the sacred river. Those who could afford it put a coin in the mouth of the deceased loved one to bribe their way into paradise. The moment the remains were dumped into the river, boys dove for the coins! The boat I hired took me right into the midst of the Ganges River bathers and into the area where the boys were diving for coins. On the sacred side of the river, people were as thick as ants, but on the side that wasn't sacred, the bank was little used. I saw many strange sights—dozens of snake charmers, men walking on spikes, even sleeping on beds of nails.

I visited the magnificent Taj Mahal, standing brilliantly in the sun, with its carved marble screens and never-to-be-forgotten architecture. I eventually saw a considerable amount of India, traversing this interesting country all the way to Bombay. Finally, we sailed on to Naples, Italy, where I left the cruise ship to tour Europe on my own.

Since many of my readers may be familiar with the sights of Europe, I'll say only that my first tour of Europe was like opening the doors to a new world. I fell in love with each country as I visited it, but France impressed me the most—even though I couldn't speak a word of French at the time!

I was very much impressed in seeing the magnificent St. Peter's Basilica, a virtual treasure chest of art and history, considered to be the finest basilica in the world; and the Vatican Museum and the Sistine Chapel, with rich displays of the works of Michelangelo and the Raphael Rooms.

During this period in the United States, Prohibition was still in effect, and by 1925 people were unhappy with it. In that year, 113,000 illegal "stills" were seized and 2,000 people died from unhealthful "bootleg" liquor. The government was being burdened as it tried to enforce the law, but more importantly, it was losing enormous amounts of revenue previously collected from the sale of liquor. These were some of the factors that eventually led to legalizing the sale of alcohol.

In 1926, Rudolph Valentino died, and I recall reading that 30,000 people attended his funeral in near hysteria. I remember vividly the year 1927 when Charles Lindbergh obtained financial backing from a group of St. Louis businessmen to compete for the $25,000 prize offered for the first nonstop solo flight between New York and Paris. Flying his famous monoplane, "Spirit of St. Louis," Lindbergh achieved that goal and was awarded the Medal of Honor. Many mothers with newborn sons named them "Lindy."

Of my many trips, the one to Alaska in August 1926 stands out. This was the year after my around-the-world tour. The ship departed from Vancouver, British Columbia, Canada, and steamed through hundreds of little jewel-like islands, all wooded to the water's edge and very beautiful. It was possible to own an island, and many people did—especially those interested in raising animals for their fur. On an island, there was no need for fences, because the animals couldn't escape.

This was a time before the introduction of sonar and radar, so skippers avoided running aground on an island in the fog or darkness by listening for the "echo" of their whistle that was blown every few seconds. Additionally, in those days boats could sail up close to the glaciers where large ice blocks, some bigger than a house, would break off and tumble into the sea. The cracking of the glaciers sounded like thunder, and the falling pieces of ice caused huge splashes, with subsequent waves so large that they could capsize a small boat.

In Fairbanks, Alaska, I met some students who were attending the university there. They had homesteaded tracts of land just outside of town, had built themselves log cabins and had stored a winter's supply of food, which they protected by hanging from tree limbs out of the reach of animals. In the dead of winter, I was told, the students would dig a tunnel in the deep snow, and that provided a "road" that enabled them to commute to school.

It was September when I left Fairbanks in a small wood-burning boat to go downstream on the Yukon River. The caribou were migrating south by the thousands. From time to time, our boat had to wait while the huge herds of caribou swam across the river. As we passed some Indian cemeteries, I asked, "Why are there big mirrors along the river?" I was told that the Indians put them up so that the spirits of the departed would know when the salmon were coming upstream.

I will always recall the warm hospitality of the people of Fairbanks. Even though I was a complete stranger, they invited me to social functions and even offered me guns and hunting equipment for my personal use.

CHAPTER SEVEN

On my return home from the Alaskan trip, I decided that, with the Mission Pak business doing so well, I should have a home of my own.

Building sites in the new subdivision overlooking Silver Lake appealed to me, so I bought a hillside lot for $6,000 cash. Then, I had an architect draw plans for a two-story, English-style home. I hired two good, dollar-an-hour carpenters, bought the material and started the work. In due course, the house was completed—with three fireplaces and a swimming pool. With the help of a good decorator, the home was soon ready for occupancy. I then sent my mother a train ticket and urged her to leave Tipton, my step-father, and come to California. She came, and I arranged for her to get a divorce from Tipton. I also arranged for her to receive a check each month, so that she would never again have economic worries.

As my businesses expanded and became more profitable, I needed to have presentable transportation. I discovered that if a person picked up a new Cadillac in Detroit, Michigan, where the cars were built, the purchase price was reduced by more than $1,000. So I arranged to take a Detroit delivery of a new car each year on my return trips from Europe.

Since I hadn't visited my hometown of Fremont, Nebraska, in years, I thought it would be nice to stop off and visit relatives and old school friends on my way home from Detroit. My relatives were happy to see me and made me welcome, but when I looked up my school friends, I got a shock.

A girl named Fairy, whom I had always thought of as the epitome of feminine grace and the ultimate in beauty, still lived in town, but she was now divorced. When I went by to see her, I could hardly believe that she was the same person I had known in childhood! Her long black hair, that I had so greatly admired, had been cut short. Instead of the rose-petal pink skin I remembered, she now appeared weatherbeaten; she was overweight, and the voice that was so velvet-toned earlier was no longer intriguing. Nevertheless, Fairy was friendly and glad to see me.

My former sidekick and pal, Ben, was farming just outside of town, I was told, so I drove out to his farm. Sure enough, there he was with a team of horses, pulling a big cultivator, heading toward me. I waved—but he kept right on cultivating. So I drove to his house and waited. Eventually, Ben came in, but it was obvious that he was uncomfortable. I tried to be friendly, but he remained cool and reserved. I suppose I should have realized that my new Cadillac convertible made him feel embarrassed and inferior, even though I never intended that to happen.

Next, I looked up Art, another of my buddies, in the phone book and called him. He remembered me all right, he said, but when I asked if we could get together, he explained that he was awfully busy at the time, but if I would call him in advance the next time I passed through, he would try to arrange it.

There was another girl in Fremont named Pearl. I remembered her, but I had never really "taken a shine to her." However, she seemed very glad to see me when we got together. She was married and had five children, but was anxious to talk about "old times." That evening after our meeting, she called me on the phone to arrange to see me again the following day. I was rather surprised that a married woman and mother of five would be so anxious to see more of me. When she came over the next day, she said she was "packed and ready to go to California" with me! And Pearl was in no mood to take "no" for an answer—so I cut my visit short and left early the next morning.

I spent my last evening in my hometown at Aunt Mary and Uncle George's house. He's the uncle for whom I had picked bugs off potato plants for a nickel a tin can. It was interesting to discuss the "good ol' days," but we were kept busy slapping mosquitoes and chiggers. I asked Uncle George if he'd ever considered screening in his porch. "No," he said matter-of-factly. "I'm used to it the way it is." It was a good lesson for me: don't try to change people!

Then, as now, young men loved sports cars. But many didn't have the means to buy an expensive new sports car, so they would buy a used Model T Ford for around $300, remove the body and have a custom, racer-type body built on the chassis. I, too, wanted a sports car, but I couldn't see paying $600 for a custom body. So, I ran a newspaper ad for a sheet metal worker. When a capable applicant responded, I asked if he could build a sports car body from scratch. "Yes, I can," he answered—and I hired him for one dollar an hour!

We made plans for what I wanted, and I bought the auto body sheet steel. Together, we made the wooden frame, then cut metal to cover it. I kept patterns of each part, and when the body was completed, I paid my sheet metal worker the $60 he had earned. That was "big money" in those days!

I then ran an ad for a young handyman. A 17-year-old Canadian lad applied, and I hired him at $1.50 for a 10-hour day. I worked with him, and together we made a duplicate of the sheet metal man's job. The auto body we built turned out passable, and we felt sure we could do better on the next one.

We started a third auto body, and by now the boy was able to go ahead without too much help from me. So, I purchased parts by the dozen and put the boy on a piece-work basis. Within a short time, he was making double his original day rate, and we were turning out a body a day. I enclosed a dust-proof area and started painting the bodies in assorted colors.

The cars needed some form of upholstering for the seats. However, a professional upholstering job ran about $45, as much as I was selling the bodies for. As luck would have it, the Day Company, an upholstering material supplier, had a fire, and almost everything in their warehouse was a loss. Fifty-inch rolls of tightly rolled imitation leather were burned— except near the ends of the rolls. There was as much as 6 to 10 inches that, when unrolled, was still in perfect condition. I offered to haul away the burned rolls for what I could salvage, and they were glad to be rid of what they considered of no value.

In my shop, I removed the burned portion on the rolls. When the unburned portion was unrolled, I had miles of expensive imitation leather in various colors. I bought a power sewing machine, hired an upholsterer and we were then able to sew the pieces together to give the effect of expensive tufted upholstery. My auto body customers were delighted to pay $15 extra for the upholstery. Later, I had cast aluminum windshield frames made, and we manufactured little tops. So, many buyers came back for the accessories.

Ford and Chevrolet Bodies "All Kinds All Prices", 810 E. 9th St., L. A.

A typical sports auto body I built by the hundreds,
1921-1928

As the business grew, I designed a second model in order to provide a choice of either a torpedo-style body or a style with a trunk in back for those who wanted to carry things.

In the beginning, I had only intended to make a speedster body for my own personal use, but when I saw how easy it was to make the bodies and how popular they were, I decided to start a new sideline business. I registered the company under the name "Star Auto Body." It turned out to be a modestly profitable sideline business. However, I never allowed it to interfere with my main business, Mission Pak. The sports car craze eventually started to quiet down, and I had an opportunity to sell Star Auto Body. When I sold the business, it left me free to look for a new sideline.

My next adventure was a business building homes. I had observed that in the developed part of south Los Angeles, there were still some vacant lots among the improved ones. The vacant lots were 60 feet wide by 140 feet deep, and the prices ran approximately $1,200. But if I split each lot, I would have room for an 800-square-foot house on each half (each 30-foot lot). That would reduce my cost for the land to $600 per house. So, I purchased the lots and let out contracts for the houses, each with a bedroom, living room, kitchen, and bath—and with hardwood floors.

My cost was two dollars per square foot, or $1,600 per house. That, plus $600 for the half-lot brought my cost to $2,200. I added $800 for a carport, landscaping and painting—so my total cost was about $3,000. I priced the houses at $3,500 and did the selling myself—$100 down and $35 a month, including 7 percent interest. I sold them on contract, "carrying the papers" myself, thus eliminating escrow charges and sales costs. The houses sold as fast as they were completed. The adventure turned out to be a successful sideline to Mission Pak.

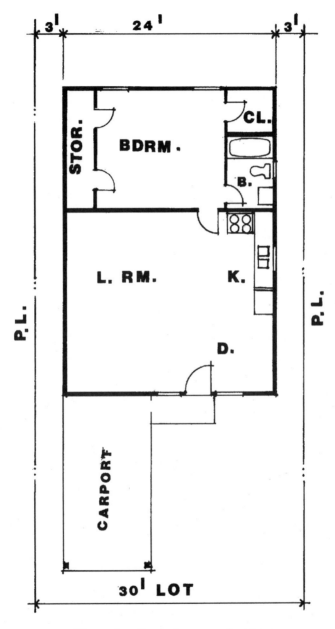

Floor plan for 800 square-foot house

As I passed the 30-year mark, my life took another dramatic turn—because at about that time I met my wife-to-be. It was the early 1930s, and the sizable French community in Los Angeles staged an annual gathering hosted by the famous actor Charles Boyer and other celebrities. I attended the event and met a lady to whom I had sold one of my houses. She, in turn, introduced me to a Miss Juliette Creste, the daughter of a French World War I veteran. I was quite impressed by Juliette and her mother, and I enjoyed chatting with the two of them. Juliette told me that she had been born in San Francisco, but that both her parents were from France. She had learned to speak French fluently in the home. As I got better acquainted with her, I realized that Juliette was truly a remarkable young lady. It wasn't long before I proposed and she accepted! The year was 1932...Juliette was 26, and I was 31.

By this time, my mother had become acquainted with Peter Wanquist, who was a building contractor. It wasn't long before they had married and decided to move into their own income-property so they could supervise it easier and more conveniently. That left the Silver Lake residence available, and eventually, my bride, Juliette, and I moved in.

We honeymooned in Oregon, driving through miles of gorgeous rhododendrons in full bloom. I was so carried away with the beauty that I picked huge bunches of rhododendrons and filled our convertible. When we stopped for gas at the next town, I found out that it was against the law to cut the rhododendrons. You can imagine how quickly I unloaded the car!

Upon our return home, I became better acquainted with Juliette's mother and found her to be delightful, too. I encouraged her to visit us in our new Silver Lake home. I respected my mother-in-law's practical, "quaint" notions. For example, she believed a girl should be brought up to know how to cook, manage a home and get along with people. Thanks to the training she provided, my wife managed our home beautifully and with grace, and I can't recall ever having a bad meal at home in our 36 years of married life. Fortunately for me, Juliette shared my love of traveling, so we enjoyed many trips together all over the globe.

We loved the view of Silver Lake from our home. And we enjoyed the three fireplaces and other features of the house. It wasn't far from downtown Los Angeles where my business was located, so it was very convenient, as well. We made it our home for 17 years.

Newly Weds

The residence in Silver Lake I built at age 37

Although my preoccupation with business limited my time for sporting events, I tried to keep up with what was going on in sports: Babe Ruth, the fantastic baseball player, had 60 homeruns in 1927; boxing champ Jack Dempsey was the first to have "million-dollar" gate receipts; Helen Will's tennis was the talk of the town; and Glenna Collett and Bobby Jones were king and queen of golf.

In October 1929, the stock market crashed, ushering in the Great Depression. Things continued to worsen, and by 1932, the people were ready for a change in the White House. In that year, Franklin D. Roosevelt was elected to the presidency. But by the time of his inauguration in March 1933, the country was near panic. Fortunately, Roosevelt took drastic action: he closed the banks, called an emergency session in congress and pushed his requested legislation through in 100 days—15 new laws that have permanently changed the American way of life! Soon the unemployed were given jobs; farmers were given crop insurance; Prohibition was repealed; home foreclosures were halted; and bank deposits were insured. After being closed four days, the banks were reopened, and deposits immediately exceeded withdrawals. Gradually, business returned to normal.

Also in 1933, the federal government called in all gold (bars and coins) at the current monetary rate of $35 an ounce. Owners of the precious metal were very upset, but they were required by law to turn in their gold or risk being fined. Eventually, the price of gold soared. I was "fortunate"—I didn't have any gold to turn in!

Following the calling in of gold, silver dollars began to be less in evidence. I reasoned that the silver dollars would appreciate in value, and I made a tour of several banks to buy as many as possible. I soon had a total of 10,000 of them. Within a year, I saw an ad in the *Los Angeles Times* that read, "Wanted, silver dollars, will pay $2.00 each." Obviously, doubling my money was a good thing, so I sold all my silver dollars. But when the price of silver skyrocketed, I realized I had sold too soon. It was an experience and a lesson concerning TIMING!

The improvement in motion picture making and the wide publicity given to movie stars caused the movie industry to boom, along with the profitable business of operating theaters. The big studios had all the top talent under contract and spared no effort or expense to create films with mass appeal. Although films were still silent, stars like Rudolph Valentino, Harold

Lloyd, Mary Pickford, Charlie Chaplin and many others were very popular with the public. Customers formed long lines at the theaters to see their favorite films.

All films were silent up to 1927. But in that year in a New York City theater, jazz singer Al Jolson, on his knees and with face smeared black, sang the immortal song "Mammy" on a sound track. So, we saw *and heard* our first talking picture. Its popularity and great success meant that all the movie studios were forced to begin making "talkies." The changeover caused much confusion—but it was what the public wanted. The actors with good speaking voices were in big demand, but some of the former silent stars that didn't have good voices were out in the cold! Although a far cry from the accomplishments of today's special effects, lighting and colossal, multimillion-dollar productions, the first talkies were very popular.

During the early '20s, my Mission Pak business boomed. However, after the stock market crash in 1929, most businesses, including Mission Pak, took a nose dive. Fortunately, I managed to "not go under." But many other businesses were not so lucky. Men who had their money in stocks, particularly those stocks bought on margin, were completely wiped out. Some were so despondent that they jumped from their office windows. Unemployment reached 25 percent, and at that time, there was no such thing as unemployment insurance, food stamps or welfare.

All went well for my real estate venture until the crash of '29—then, one by one, my home buyers lost their jobs and were unable to make their payments. So, like other builders, I had repossessions and vacancies on my hands. Most of the other builders would immediately shut off the water in order to save expenses. But soon, as the lawn died and weeds grew up, kids would break the windows, and thieves would steal the plumbing fixtures. Their homes became shambles.

I decided on a different course. I hired a tract gardener to maintain the lawns and shrubs. Then I ran an ad in the newspaper that read, "For Rent, one-bedroom new cottages, $15 a month, including gardener, to senior citizens only." In a short time, my vacant houses were occupied, and the senior citizens took good care of the properties. At the end of three years, with attractive lawns and shrubs, the homes sold for more than I had asked originally.

This was only one of several times in my life when the outlook was discouraging. However, I discovered that by concentrating on a solution, in most cases a way can be found to weather the storm and come out all right!

Not long ago, I took a tour of those houses that I had built some 60 years earlier. I wanted to see what they looked like today. With one exception, they were all rented, and I was told that the monthly rents were running nearly ten times the original purchase payments I had asked.

On one of my trips to France, I saw candied fruit in a confection store window, and I thought how nice it would be for variety in my Mission Pak baskets. I learned that the candied fruit was made in the town of Grass, in the south of France. I went there and managed to learn how they made the confection. On my return to the United States, I experimented and found an easier and faster method—which I used to make tons of candied cherries, tangerines, pineapples, apricots and other fruits. When sugar was rationed during the war, I substituted honey and found that it made an even better product. At one time, I had most of the bees in California working for me!

In Japan, 1936

CHAPTER NINE

Before World War II, I would go abroad annually to buy garnishments and containers for the business. When the war broke out and I learned that my boatload of containers from Japan couldn't be delivered, I called my insurance agent and asked for payment on my "War Risk Policy." He suggested I read the fine print on the back of my policy that stated that the ship had to be lost on the "high seas" in order to be entitled to a settlement. Then, 20 years later, I received a letter from the Japanese government, with a check for the amount covered by the policy. My wife and I celebrated the windfall and took another trip abroad!

During my 34 years in Mission Pak, I had a number of shocks and disappointments, but aside from the loss of my boatload of Japanese containers, there was none that put butterflies swirling in my insides like the following incident:

Among the many stores we would rent each year, there were always some with more windows than we needed for display. We solved the problem by having large colorful photos of fruit printed on paper. We then cut out the huge pineapples, oranges, pears and other items and affixed them on the inside of windows to fill up space, thereby reducing the area needed for displaying merchandise. When the lights inside the store shone through the photos of the fruit, it was very eye-catching and gave us immediate recognition. However, we had difficulty attaching the photo paper to the glass; the Scotch tape we first tried came loose under the heat of the floodlights. A display shop sold me a gallon can of adhesive for pasting paper on glass that worked perfectly. So, we used it on the windows of all our stores from San Diego to Sacramento.

At the close of the season, we washed the windows of the stores before returning the keys as a routine matter. But we quickly found that when we removed the printed fruit, the glass was etched by the adhesive. Well, I was sick...because I was responsible for the windows that we had damaged, and plate glass was expensive. I decided that we would keep quiet, but if the landlord of any of the stores complained, we would replace the glass at that time. And some owners did complain within a few days. I had never been so worried, because we had no insurance for such a problem, and replacing the glass in all the stores probably would mean financial ruin for me.

Luckily, a boatload of Belgian plate glass arrived at just that time, creating a temporary glut in the local plate glass market. So, I was able to replace the glass at surprisingly low prices. I was especially concerned about the large block-long department store I had rented in Long Beach. Replacing all the glass in that enormous building would have meant disaster for sure. To my surprise, a new tenant took over the store shortly after we vacated and removed all the windows for remodeling. In a number of other cases, remodeling also followed our leaving, and I wasn't asked to pay for the damages. At the end of the month, I was greatly relieved to know that I had only been obligated to replace about $37,000 worth of plate glass.

I sued the seller of the adhesive, and in time I was reimbursed for all I had paid out to replace the damaged glass. The moral of the story is: even in the most hopeless-appearing situations, by keeping calm, one can often end up without being damaged too badly! Of course, I wasn't compensated for my worry or loss of sleep, but I did get back the cash I had spent to correct the situation. And incidently, replacing the glass created goodwill with the landlords, making it easier for me to rent stores in future years.

Just to anticipate and schedule the delivery of the thousands of things required for the complex Mission Pak business was mind-boggling. Making all the things we sold required a 90,000-square-foot packing plant and a crew of 800 trained people working two shifts. In advance of the holiday season, I would tour the entire State of California by car looking for desirably located, vacant stores. Each possibility required the name of the owner and a sketch of the facility with dimensions, along with the style and size of the windows and the condition of the floor. I would then estimate the expected sales and determined what rental fee was justified. From my years in the business, I was able to judge the potential fairly closely. Once the location was deemed feasible, then came the exhausting negotiations with the owners. I would have to overcome their objections to renting on a temporary basis and their set notions of high rental fees.

Like an athlete in training, I built myself up physically in advance of each season so that I could carry the load and work the long hours for that hectic 60 days. Along with everything else required to manage the business, I also personally negotiated all store rentals.

I expanded and became more efficient in handling the volume with each year in the business. More former employees were available each season, and that made it much easier. People would sometimes ask, "How can you find enough artistic people to create those lovely gift baskets and boxes?" The secret was that we simplified the procedures on each of the assembly line conveyors. Each operator's part was simple, and even an unskilled person could be trained within minutes to do the routine individual operations. Each procedure in my shipping room was also simplified and, where possible, minimized. And in every case, things were made easy. For example, the order books used in the stores were so designed that the original copy of the order form, where the customer filled in the name and address of the intended recipient, became the shipping label. This had several advantages. We avoided making mistakes in copying the information, we saved time typing labels and, when the package reached its destination, the local postman was better qualified to interpret the ambiguous letters or figures that might apply to his area.

Each type of gift pack had a "model number," and that number was added to the order/label when the customer selected a certain gift pack. That number, which appeared on the corner of the label, enabled us to sort the labels by pack model, and, since we knew the gross weight of each type of pack, we could add the necessary postage stamps to the original label. Therefore, when a sorted stack of labels arrived in the shipping room, it was only a matter of pulling those packs from the shelves, attaching the labels and dispatching the gift packs on our trucks to the post office. All shipments were prepaid and made from my Los Angeles packing plant. Every morning, we collected the orders from all the stores and processed them without delay. Each store deposited its sales cash daily in a local bank.

During the season, my employees would sometimes number more than 1,000. I found women to be more dependable than men, so mostly I hired women, both in the packing plant and in the stores.

The ladies we recruited for our sales staff in the stores were requested to attend our sales training school for two days, for which they were paid. We rented an auditorium and set up a model store on the stage. I personally demonstrated the salient features that a sales person should apply in her daily contact with customers. Most importantly, I brought out the fact that the sales person should always *smile* and greet the customers warmly when they entered the store. I taught the sales staff that if they were asked, "How much is this?" they should say, "This lovely gift will be delivered anywhere in the United States, postpaid, for only three fifty"—never "three dollars and fifty cents!" If they were asked, "What's in the bottom of the basket?" I suggested the sales person answer, "Every basket is packed solid to the bottom with more of the delicious fruits and nuts you see on the top." In response to "Well, suppose my shipment arrives damaged?" the sales force was taught to respond, "Every shipment we make is guaranteed to be delivered in good condition, and if not, we will replace it or refund your money." If someone objected, "The oranges might freeze!" the sales people were to answer, "No, all our fresh fruits are sent in heated express cars, so we can guarantee that they will arrive in good condition." If the customer asked, "How can I be sure?" we were to answer, "Mission Pak has been in business since 1918, and we stand behind every order." If the customer persisted with "Yes, but you close after Christmas," our response was to be, "That is true, we do close this store. However, our permanent office address and phone number are on your receipt."

On and on the training session went, with potential questions and suggested answers: "Tell me exactly what's underneath"—"Gladly, here is a list of each item it contains. Can't you just see the joy your Boston friends will experience when they open this colorful gift from California? You couldn't possibly remember them in a nicer way." "Well, it seems rather expensive"—"Not when you consider that we prepay and insure. And it will be something different. They will put your gift under their Christmas tree and, believe me, it will steal the show....Be enthusiastic and *smile, smile, smile!*"

"When the customer tells you where they want to ship the gift pack," I told my future sales people, "smile and say enthusiastically, 'Oh my, I can just see the way their faces will light up back in Kansas (or wherever) when they receive a gift like this all the way from California! Undoubtedly, they will write and tell you how much they appreciate your thoughtfulness.'"

As a part of the sales program, I asked that each sales person familiarize herself with the different gift packs so she could describe them in detail. "When the matter of 'weight' is brought up," I told them, "never stress *pounds*. We can't compete with markets that sell by the pound. Instead, say, 'The lovely pack is a full two pounds *net*, but, of course, much more packed for shipping—and remember, we prepay the postage and insurance.'" I suggested that when a customer was rude, surly or sarcastic, just *smile!* And pretend not to notice.

And so it went—for two days—at the end of which we had a question and answer period. That was followed by a graduation ceremony where each student was given a diploma and a check for two days pay.

The ladies were assigned to specific stores. But before starting work, each was given orange smocks, a change belt and some change. In the case of stores outside Los Angeles, they were instructed that each night they were to send in their orders by Greyhound bus; their sales cash was to be deposited in a local bank. On the whole, the simple system worked out surprisingly well, and the salary, plus commission, made the work so profitable that many ladies returned to work year after year.

CHAPTER TEN

On my first visit to France back in 1925, I had fallen in love with the country, the people and the food. I had found that I enjoyed everything about it, even though I didn't speak a word of French, and I decided that it would be even more enjoyable if I could communicate. After several more visits, I decided I simply had to learn to speak the language. I was 28 years old by that time.

It became possible for me to spend a full month in France, so I employed a full-time student at the Sorbonne, an English major, as my French teacher. I didn't have the patience to start by mastering all the conjugations. Instead, I decided to learn like the French children do. I knew how fluent the children quickly became, so I just stocked up on French children's books.

On the first day with my teacher, Miss Pevai, I asked that she read aloud the first page of *The Three Bears*. I repeated as she read, and she corrected me. We rehearsed until I could read and understand page one. We turned the page and repeated the process—and so on until we finished *The Three Bears*; then we moved on to *Cinderella* and followed the same learning procedure.

It wasn't long until we had moved on to French newspapers and then to novels. The margins of the pages of the papers and books I read became filled with scribbled translations, but little by little I was able to communicate in French. I made countless mistakes as I learned, and I still do today! I'm sure I will never master the proper conjugations or genders, but I am understood by the French people, and they are considerate when I make mistakes. Never in all my visits to France have I ever been mistreated. On the contrary, I have experienced many courtesies and kindnesses.

On one of those early trips to France, I saw cellophane being used to wrap bottles of perfume in Paris. It was a new product at that time, and I thought, "What a fantastic product, and how wonderful it would be on my Mission Pak gift packs." I learned where it was being manufactured, bought a sizable quantity and brought it home. It worked out just as I thought it would. The public was fascinated to see my gift packs wrapped in "unbreakable glass," as some were calling the product. People were anxious to touch it—they were fascinated by a product that looked like glass, yet could be curved, bent or folded without breaking. From that time on, I used it on all my fruit baskets and in other ways.

In London, 1950

"Hindsight," as they say, "is always 20/20." I later realized that I should have applied for an exclusive franchise to distribute cellophane in the United States. Because at that time, waxed paper was the only thing companies had as wrappers for chewing gum, cigarettes, and many other products.

On our annual trips abroad, my wife, Juliette, and I were constantly on the look-out for new ideas in packaging and garnishments, or any idea that we thought would enhance the sales in our Mission Pak business. Upon our return from trips, we would spend days in our designing room trying new ideas and innovations and different concepts in packaging. After all, we had the same basics—fruits and nuts—always fresh, the very best and of highest quality; however, in novel ways, each year packages appeared differently attractive.

While traveling in Japan, we got helpful ideas for colorful packaging. In France, we observed the colorful garnishments along with novel ribbon-design accessories.

Juliette and I would consolidate the salient features and come up with our own version of new, unique ideas for packaging. Then, I would take over the "mechanics" of how to implement the new ideas particularly for shipping so that any "rough handling" in shipment would not damage the appearance of the contents. By use of "die-cut" cardboard, I could protect the contents and make sure it would and could take any rough handling and, most importantly, arrive at its destination with the ribbon-bow uncrushed and beautiful to behold in the eyes of the recipient. In this manner, we achieved our objectives: (1) That the package would arrive on time, (2) with great "eye-appeal", and (3) that the quality of the contents would also satisfy the "taste appeal" of the recipients.

Juliette and I both enjoyed traveling, so we continued to make trips abroad each year. For me, travel was and is the most rewarding form of recreation that I have found, next to reading.

Juliette with a Mission Pak display

Travel, however, was quite different in the old days. Beginning in California, the four-day trip across the United States by railway was without air conditioning—open windows let in dust and cinders from the coal-burning locomotive. But we didn't seem to mind. At mealtime, we would pass from car to car in order to reach the diner, where white-gloved waiters were ready to serve us a very delicious meal. The brook trout in Idaho was a treat, and the Kansas City prime beef was delicious. Typically, when we finally reached New York City, we stayed at one of the big hotels for several days before sailing time. During that time, we enjoyed the various Broadway shows and musicals. On sailing day, we took a taxi to the harbor—with our big steamer trunk in tow, for we had to be prepared to dress for dinner each night (and a lady must have changes...with shoes to match!). The huge ocean liners—the *Queen Mary*, the *United States*, the *Beringaria*, the *Isle de France* and others—were all floating palaces, with shops, swimming pools, gyms, beauty salons, masseuses and every convenience.

At night there was always a good orchestra and dancing. When we crossed on the *United States*, it was not unusual to travel with the Duke and Duchess of Windsor. After docking on the coast of France, we took the boat-train to Paris, and after more excitement, we would be deposited in one of the lovely hotels. Like most women, my wife loved to shop, and when she got to know designer Pierre Cardin, he made her special deals on experimental designs that were too costly to reproduce. Some were reversible, and all were handmade evening gowns that today would cost thousands. Pierre let my wife have them for a few hundred. To be sure, our trunk was packed full when we returned.

Two major events happened in 1941. First, the miracle drug penicillin was discovered. Since then, it has saved millions of lives. I can't help but reflect that, in 1906 when my father was injured in an accident and septicemia (blood poisoning) set in, he died for lack of penicillin, and I had to grow up without a father.

Secondly, on December 7, 1941, I was in San Francisco on a business tour of my Mission Pak stores when the shocking news hit the headlines: "Pearl Harbor Attacked by Japan." The surprise attack stunned everyone. President Roosevelt lost no time in calling for Congress to declare war on Japan, knowing that it would also mean war with Germany. The speculation was over; we were really at war. I was a little old for the draft, but I did want to support the war effort for my country. But what could I do to help?

Government representatives contacted me and said, "We need you to operate a food plant. Our troops need nonperishable food desperately, and your packing plant could be converted to a dehydration plant. We'll send you to Berkeley and teach you how to dehydrate vegetables."

So I went to Berkeley and came back knowing how to dehydrate vegetables, and the government was ready with a contract for many tons of food. However, they couldn't give me a priority to buy new equipment. I had to tour the state and pick up used equipment, piece by piece. I located a large boiler, and, with the help of handy craftsmen, we made a dehydration heat tunnel where the trays of vegetables traveled along in a current of hot air. Each piece of vegetable was reduced in size and weight as the water evaporated. And the food became both nonperishable and lightweight. Just what the government wanted!

In advance, I had contracted with growers from San Diego to Sacramento to produce crops of carrots. In some cases, the farmers were paid as much as the land had cost them for just one season's crop.

My equipment worked well, and we were soon turning out hundreds of five gallon cans of dehydrated vegetables—mainly carrots. When cooked in water with a little butter and seasoning, the reconstituted vegetables were no different than freshly prepared ones. However, when Army cooks prepared them with river water and with no seasoning, the men came to hate the large portions of dehydrated vegetables. I learned never to mention that I had made dehydrated vegetables to returning servicemen!

A lot of our carrots were shipped to Russia, and I never heard how it worked out in their borscht. I did hear one story about a cook opening a five-gallon can of our carrots in the humid South Pacific. That's enough for 200 men, but there were only ten in their group, so the cook removed only a small amount from the can. That night the opened can with the remaining carrots, exposed to the warmth and humidity, overflowed all over the kitchen with expanding carrots.

All during the war, the government kept pressing me for more production, so I began running two shifts. In addition to a double shift for the dehydration operation, I continued to also operate my Mission Pak business, but on a reduced scale. It meant long hours for me, but I was used to that. Getting help for Mission Pak was a serious problem, because the aircraft industry was employing every available able-bodied person for their assembly lines, even grandmothers. My Mission Pak stores managed with middle-aged ladies, and the packing plant and dehydration operation used minorities, most of whom didn't speak English. However, with bilingual supervisors, we were able to accommodate our Mission Pak customers and, at the same time, turn out tons of dehydrated products for the war effort.

The high point in the war came on June 6, 1944, when General Dwight D. Eisenhower, Commander of the Allied Forces, gave the order and the troops crossed the English Channel to France. In the surprise attack, the Germans put up a terrific fight that cost many lives, but the Allied Forces gradually occupied most of France. They then pushed on, over the Rhine, until they reached Berlin, and Germany formally surrendered.

The United States, however, still had Japan to deal with. When the Japanese destroyed much of our Naval power at Pearl Harbor, they were able to control the Pacific, seizing Guam, Wake,

Hong Kong, Indonesia and, most agonizing for America, the Philippines. With Naval replacements, we were gradually able to retake the Philippines and the South Pacific islands, one by one. We were still faced with the problem of defeating mainland Japan and knew it would cost thousands of lives. To save those lives and bring the war to an end, President Harry S. Truman decided to use a newly developed weapon—the atomic bomb.

When the first atomic bomb was dropped on Hiroshima, it didn't convince the Japanese. A second bomb was then dropped on Nagasaki, and that brought the desired results. Japan formally surrendered at an historic ceremony, with General Douglas MacArthur presiding over the meeting aboard the battleship *Missouri*.

Following the defeat of Japan and the end of World War II, the United States enjoyed international respect and was envied as the richest and most powerful country on earth. We thought we had a monopoly on making the atomic bomb. Consequently, we started to disarm and reduce our armed forces and relax. But on September 23, 1949, we were shocked to learn that the Soviets had exploded their own atomic bomb. Now we no longer had the terrible weapon to ourselves, and we had reason to believe that the Soviet Union was determined to force its Communist system on the rest of the world. Our government started preparing to defend the United States when war came, and many of our citizens got into the act by digging underground shelters to be ready when the bombs fell. This was the beginning of our costly military build-up, the beginning of the "Cold War" with the U.S.S.R.—and sadly, billions of dollars were added to our budget deficit.

The Family

Returning from Europe on the *United States*

CHAPTER ELEVEN

The day World War II was over, the government no longer wanted dehydrated vegetables. Soon, an inspector paid me a visit and asked to see a sample of my carrots. He spread a black cloth on a table, dumped some of my carrots on the black cloth and started moving the pieces around with his stick. He shook his head. "Sorry," he said. "Too many imperfect cubes."

I asked him how he expected me to have only cubes from *round* carrots. "That's your problem," he replied without expression. "We can't use your carrots anymore."

So I was stuck with a small mountain of five gallon cans of dehydrated carrots. With no market for the product, I was worried. When a baker friend of mine learned of my problem, he asked me to give him some of the carrots to experiment with. In a few days, he was back with a beautiful pumpkin pie. "It's nice, but why bring me a pumpkin pie?" I said. He asked me to taste it. "It's delicious," was my response.

"Well, it's never seen a pumpkin," said the baker. "It's made from your carrots!"

After another few days, my friend returned with a carrot cake, and everyone agreed it was delicious! The news spread fast, and before long, I had sold every can of carrots to bakeries across the country. In fact, they wanted even more, but I was sold out. By this time, I had even dismantled my dehydrating equipment. But I've often wondered if that could have been the beginning of the now popular "carrot cake!" The unharvested crops of carrots I had contracted, all went to seed. Finally, I sold the carrot seeds for bird seed.

All through the war, I had continued my Mission Pak operation on a reduced scale. Now I was eager to go all out—and when I did, the business boomed!

I was approached by two men who wanted to buy the company. I thought it over seriously...I had been sole owner and operator of the company for 34 years. But I finally decided I needed a change, so I sold Mission Pak—the trade name, the real estate, the entire business. I agreed to stay on in an advisory capacity for two years at $50,000 a year. I lived up to my part of the bargain and the buyers to theirs. By the second year, they were able to carry on alone. After I sold Mission Pak, my wife and I moved to Malibu.

In the months that followed the disastrous attack on Pearl Harbor, many people were afraid the "Japs," as they were called then, would invade our California coast, so beach property values were depressed. Consequently, I bought 30-foot-wide beach front lots at $30 a running foot as they became available. After a few years, I sold them for $300 a running foot—a ten-fold profit. I thought I was pretty smart! But time has proved how wrong I was: the lots are now valued at $6,000 a running foot—and higher! However, I suppose it's good to remember that a profit is only a profit when you take it.

While searching for beach lots between Santa Monica and Malibu, I came upon a beach home with a "For Sale" sign on it. It was built around some huge rocks, with boulders under the house and more on the ocean front. The property was run-down, but I could see how, with work, it could be made livable and attractive. So, I asked the price. As was my custom, regardless of the quoted price, I said, "Too high. But I might be interested at a lower price." In the end, the owner brought his price down, and I bought the house, with 120 feet of beach front, at a reasonable price.

In time, with lots of repair and remodeling, the property became a showplace and was featured on the color cover of *House Beautiful* magazine, with six pages of interior photos. The large boulders on the beach side protected the house from storms, and they also provided a place for the seals to park and bark when we

100 Autobiography of George Charles Page

played music. Eventually, the sea gulls became so friendly that they took food from our fingers.

Our house guests loved the cozy lower apartment that opened onto the beach. With its tiny kitchen, guests were able to get up when they liked and prepare their own breakfast. A second downstairs apartment made comfortable quarters for our domestic help. Our guests joined my wife and me upstairs for lunch and dinner— and what banquets we had! Neighbor boys would dive off our beach and bring up lobsters that I boiled outside on the patio, split open and served with browned butter. Never have I tasted lobsters as good anywhere else.

Walks on the beach were always enjoyable, and when it rained, the rainbows over the ocean were something to behold. The sunsets were also spectacularly beautiful. I swam in the ocean every day and enjoyed my surfboard.

My wife and I each had a horse, and we used to love riding with neighbors along the beach and all over the wild Malibu hills. The deer we passed were tame, because they had never been shot at by hunters. As I reflect back on our 17 years of living on Malibu beach, I'm convinced they were the happiest years of our lives.

My wife didn't want a housekeeper for our Malibu home, but we did need someone to wash windows and do a few other chores. We heard about a married student who wanted to work part time in exchange for the use of an apartment. We agreed on an arrangement that worked well for him until he graduated. For our part, we got a handy young man who gladly gave us part-time services in exchange for living in the apartment. As one young man would graduate, we would find another. I hear from these young people periodically, and some of them now have important positions in industry. One young man, for example, now operates a very successful construction business in Las Vegas.

In 1950, my wife and I took our first trip to Europe following the conclusion of the War. The devastation was appalling. However, shops in London were open again. One big department store continued to carry on business by simply putting little fences around the huge 30-foot hole that a bomb had ripped open in its roof and down through each of its floors.

With the postwar rationing, even at the Savoy Hotel in London, we could only get two eggs a week and no meat—except fish and rabbit. As we passed Simpson's Restaurant, where before the war they had the best meat in London, we noticed they were still using the large silver carts and ceremoniously lifting the cover to serve the food in their traditional manner. "Could it be possible that Simpson's has meat?" we wondered. We went in to see. The service was as elegant as ever, but under one silver cover was a big fish and under the other was a large Australian jack rabbit!

Too young to "rock and whittle" in retirement after the sale of Mission Pak, I decided to become involved in industrial property. I bought a 60-acre corner property at Crenshaw and El Segundo boulevards in the City of Hawthorne. It was a duck pond in the winter. But I negotiated with some Los Angeles developers to deliver their fill dirt to the property. Gradually, the level of the land was raised by two feet. Then I went to a lot of trouble to have a spur railroad track brought in.

I had a subdivision map drawn, dividing the land into 5 and 10 acre parcels. In Vernon, where most industrial buildings were being built at that time, they rarely provided parking space for cars. Employees came by bus or streetcar. But in my parcels, I wanted each building to have room for parking.

The well laid out building sites were put up for sale, with paved streets and street lighting— but I had no takers. "Well," I thought, "home builders start things by building several model houses. So, why not build several industrial buildings—a 10,000-, a 20,000-, and a 30,000-square-foot facility?" They were hardly constructed when defense contractors wanted to rent them on a one- or two-year lease.

My banker-advisors shook their heads. "No, you must get longer leases; the longer the better", they said. Well, when I couldn't get longer leases, I agreed to shorter ones.

North American Aviation Company (which eventually became known as North American Rockwell, then simply Rockwell) wanted to lease a larger building, so I built a 100,000-square-foot structure for them at a rental of a nickel a square-foot for 10 years. This 10-year lease was my banker-advisor's idea of perfection. Ten years later, this transaction stood out in my record book as the poorest and least profitable of all my numerous lease deals.

I gradually built on all my land and had blue-chip tenants in every building. What a "sweetheart" of a business compared with my hectic Mission Pak fruit-packing business...more profitable and so much easier! And by the way, my tenants got their merchandise by truck and shipped by truck, so the spur track I had worked so hard to get was never used.

My industrial development proved to be a great success. As I've noted, I had a number of buildings ranging in size from 10,000-square-feet to 100,000-square-feet, and they were leased to leading aircraft and electronics firms. My net worth had now surpassed even my wildest dreams. With my ownership of large pieces of vacant land zoned for industry and with the banks eager to loan me money, I could easily have doubled my holdings and doubled my net worth within a few years, I felt quite certain. The average man would probably have jumped at such an opportunity. But I asked myself, "Would doubling my net worth add to my joy of living?"

As I thought about it, I realized that I wasn't interested in more than one home and didn't want a yacht or a string of race horses. I could sleep in only one bed and eat only three meals a day. So, after conscientiously considering various facets of the pros and cons, I made one of the most serious decisions of my life. I decided that I had all the buildings I wanted and that I was content with my net worth. Therefore, I terminated my lucrative industrial business and let a young leasing agent take my place. In order to help him get started, I advanced the commissions to him for making leases that weren't even due for several years. Consequently, he took over and operated as I had—and eventually, he became a rich man, with a number of high-rise holdings at the airport. It gave me pleasure to see him succeed, and never once have I regretted my decision to be satisfied with "well enough." I am simply not one of those men who are determined to be the richest man in the cemetery!

My Hawthorne industrial park in 1960

CHAPTER TWELVE

Against the advice of French General Charles deGaulle, our nation became involved in a tragic war with Vietnam in 1965. Our justification was that if Vietnam was overrun by the Communists, the rest of the countries in Southeast Asia would follow like dominoes. History has proven that we gained nothing by the war, but we paid for our mistake with more than 50,000 dead and at least twice that number wounded—some with permanent injuries. Many of our young men returned home addicted to drugs, and, unfortunately, the United States lost much of the international respect it had enjoyed before its disastrous blunder.

It was about this time that my wife and I decided to place the "lion's share" of our assets into a nonprofit foundation. We called it "Incentive Aid Foundation," and through it, we hoped to help students through difficult crises with gifts of cash.

We had just gotten well under way, helping students who were in financial difficulties, when the Internal Revenue Service issued a new rule

that prohibited private foundations from making
direct contributions to individuals, for fear that
they might be influenced by race, creed or color.
After that rule, the only way we could help
students was through a university, and that
robbed it of any personal relationship. So, we
started looking for another worthy cause. The
aged were suggested, and we visited a number of
homes for the elderly. But we were so
discouraged by the apathy and helplessness of
the residents that our search went on.

Then we heard about Children's Hospital of
Los Angeles. We visited and saw children who
entered the hospital with every conceivable
illness but who, after a short stay, left in good
health with a lifetime to benefit from what had
been done for them. This appealed to us and
made quite an impact on our desire to be
involved. We saw a plastic surgeon correct birth
defects, cleft palates, speech defects and so on.
We saw one little fellow have his malformed ears
corrected in minutes. In addition, we saw tiny
infants undergo surgery to correct abdominal
problems. All these things confirmed our desire
to be involved and help financially. We were sold
on Children's Hospital as a deserving cause.

We learned that Children's Hospital was
desperately in need of more parking space and
that they had problems finding living quarters
for residents, interns and nurses, where children
were accepted. Some of these staff members had
to commute by bus from the other side of town.

Fortunately, the hospital owned a sizable
parcel of land in Los Angeles on Sunset

Boulevard opposite the hospital. I arranged to have a multifloor parking structure built on the Sunset frontage, with a large thrift shop on the ground floor. Moving the thrift shop to the new structure relieved the hospital's cramped space on Vermont. As expected, the new larger thrift shop, with big windows facing Sunset Boulevard, does a much larger volume of sales—thanks also to the loyal staff and able management of Mrs. John (Anne) Wilson. The proceeds from the thrift shop are now a dependable source of income for Children's Hospital. The upper floors provide spaces that help to meet the hospital's parking needs.

On the back part of the property, behind the thrift shop and parking structure, I financed the design and construction of a multiunit apartment complex for the hospital's interns, residents and nurses. The complex included a recreation area and a laundry room on the ground floor. Needless to say, the staff members were delighted with the new quarters and lost no time moving in. I fenced in the remaining unused land for a children's play yard with sandboxes, teeter-totters, swings and little play horses for the children to ride on.

Mary Duque was a major volunteer with the hospital for more than 40 years. She was on the board of directors, and at one time was president of the board. She began the gift shop there and even paid the employees' salaries from her own pocket. Her influence was profound, especially in fund-raising. Mary's brother, Harold McAlister, left a generous contribution in his will to the hospital for the construction of a high-rise building at the corner of Sunset and Vermont. His contribution covered the cost of the new structure, but there was nothing left over to provide a 200-space parking facility, so the project was at a standstill. The building department wouldn't give permission for the McAlister building to be built until the parking places were provided. Of course, donors are reluctant to contribute to the construction of a garage. It lacks glamor!

To solve the problem and make Mary Duque happy, I investigated and found that, by tearing down a row of old houses along the west wall of the hospital's garage, I could build a multi-floor addition to the garage that would provide the extra 200 spaces. I received no recognition for the million dollars it cost me to do it, but at least the McAlister Building could then be built.

When the Children's Hospital facility on Sunset Boulevard needed a multi-floor main entry building, I covered the cost and that structure carries my name. When the hospital needed a special new million-dollar X-ray machine, I supplied it. And when a parcel of land desirable for hospital expansion became available, I contributed the money to buy it. The increasing need for the hospital's services made more space and equipment a must, and I was thankful to be in a position to help such a worthy cause.

Among the many hospital cases in which I have been involved, some stand out in my memory. For example, I remember the young married couple who finally had the baby they wanted so desperately. Unfortunately, the new baby boy could not be nursed or function in a normal manner. Each day, the baby lost weight, and after four days without nourishment or bowel function, he was sure to die. In desperation the young parents came to me for help. I arranged for the infant to be taken to Children's Hospital, with the request that the doctors try to save the baby's life. Dr. Morton M. Woolley, head of the department of surgery, took charge and determined that the cause was an internal obstruction. He operated and found that the baby's stomach was misplaced, crowding the lung area. In addition, the intestines were so twisted that the child couldn't take nourishment or function normally. With the help of powerful magnifying glasses, Dr. Woolley untangled and put in order the small intestine and the colon. Shortly after the operation, the infant started nursing and was soon functioning in a normal manner. He began to gain weight and strength. To say that his parents were ecstatic with joy would be an understatement.

The family now lives in Washington, D.C., and while in the capital recently, I paid them a visit. It was a source of true pleasure for me to see that the frail infant has now grown into a normal, healthy boy of eight. To have had a part in saving this child's life continues to give me deep satisfaction, joy and happiness.

I also remember when 8-year-old Danny Stup of Manhattan Beach was run over by a truck and both his legs were badly crushed. He was also injured internally, and his skull was fractured. For nearly three weeks, Danny lay unconscious in the Hawthorne Community Hospital. His parents, after exhausting their own means and all that they could beg and borrow from others, were very discouraged and distraught. The doctor advised amputating both legs, since putting the fragments together would take months and be very costly.

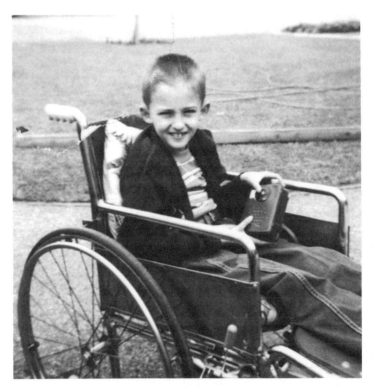

Danny Stup

Danny's mother was absolutely beside herself. She couldn't stand the thought of her son going through life without legs! The situation was brought to my attention and, after I visited Danny in the hospital and talked with his mother, I conferred with the top surgeon. He explained that it was quite possible that Danny's legs could be saved, if someone could pay not only the surgeon's fees, but also the hospital costs as well. I couldn't say no to the pleading of Danny's mother. Through lengthy procedures, Danny's legs were saved. He learned to walk again and, in time, became a Boy Scout. His mother was so grateful that she has sent me repeated thank you notes, together with progress pictures. When I last heard from him, Danny had passed the rigid physical examination and had enlisted in the U.S. Navy.

As I think about children, another story comes to mind. During World War II, the aircraft plants ran at full capacity—many had double shifts. To encourage faster production, the government let the companies operate on a "cost-plus" basis, and in their desperation for help, they hired almost every applicant. Even grandmothers worked on the assembly lines. Often, both the husband and the wife were employed, with no one to look after their children. There was a need for a facility that would provide recreation for the unattended children in the city of Hawthorne where my industrial properties were located—and when this need was brought to my attention, I provided a youth recreation center. It was very popular with the kids and their working parents. Eventually, the city leaders also realized the dire need and provided a larger facility with supervision. When I saw that the need had been addressed, I closed my youth center. But the people of Hawthorne knew of my interest in helping children, so they continued to come to me with their problems—and where I could, I helped.

Danny in uniform

CHAPTER THIRTEEN

I n the 1960s, it seems to have been, in the words of Charles Dickens, "the best of times" and "the worst of times" for our country. First, on November 22, 1963, President John F. Kennedy was assassinated in Dallas, Texas. Throughout the land, there was an overwhelming emotion of deep personal sorrow. Second, in April 1968, civil rights leader Martin Luther King, Jr., was killed by an ex-convict in Memphis, Tennessee. And, third, two months after King was shot, in June 1968, Senator Robert F. Kennedy fell under the bullet of an assassin in Los Angeles.

Between these traumatic assassinations, from 1964 to 1967, riots involving primarily blacks broke out in 58 American cities, leaving 141 dead and 4,552 injured. The riots were generally spontaneous outbursts and involved great animosity towards the police. Unless solutions are found for the social situations that spawned such violent demonstrations, there will likely be more riots. Every effort should be made to find a way for peace and harmony to prevail in our great country. I share the shame and humiliation for these criminal acts with many other people.

On the other hand, what a privilege to live in an era when we were able to see truly historic events on our television sets. On July 20, 1969, our daring astronauts actually landed and walked on the moon! What an achievement—not only to travel to and orbit the moon, but also to walk on its surface and return safely to Earth! We learned that the astronauts had even taken along a small powered vehicle to travel on the moon's surface—and collect moon rocks! It was, indeed, a "first" and something that all Americans can take pride in. As I write this a quarter of a century later, the series of Apollo explorations are still the first and only times humans have set foot on the moon.

After 36 wonderful years together, I lost my dear wife, Juliette, to cancer in 1968. When the adjustment to her death proved difficult for me, a friend suggested that a change of surroundings might help to get my mind off my troubles. I took his advice...and booked passage to Australia.

On the way there, I stopped at Tahiti and was charmed by the lovely beach and hotel at Bora-Bora. I was also greatly impressed by the variety and color of the underwater coral gardens nearby.

Moving on, the next stop was New Zealand. Although it was fall in North America, it was spring "down under," and the countryside was a lush green, spotted by multitudes of snow-white sheep. There were many things of interest to see that kept me busy, but what fascinated me most was the rain forest. Down near the southern tip of New Zealand, it's much cooler, and it gets heavy rainfall. In the moist and swampy rain forest, every twig, branch and trunk of every tree is covered with a rich green-gold moss that gives the forest a fairyland aura.

When I arrived in Australia, I met a young Australian man who told me of several things I shouldn't miss in his country. Outstanding, he said, was their unique water project, on which their government had been working for years and was spending billions of dollars. He explained that the mountain ridge that runs along the east coast traps the clouds and causes the precipitation to fall mostly along the east side. Very little moisture gets over the mountains, leaving the thousands of fertile acres of land west of the ridge very dry. Australian engineers are building a series of dams in the mountains to catch the rain so that, instead of running down to the ocean along the east coast, the rainwater can be stored in reservoirs. When completed, the reservoirs, with controlled outlets, will be connected and drained into a tunnel that will go through the mountains into the dry western side. There, the collected water will be used for irrigation. As the water passes down through the tunnel, it will turn electric turbines to generate electricity for the eastern cities.

With it being Australian springtime, the jacaranda trees were in full bloom, creating lavender bouquets everywhere, accented by splashes of color from many kinds of flowers. Of course, I was anxious to see a platypus...and to play with a koala bear...and to see how high the kangaroos could jump. After I had satisfied my curiosity on these matters, I returned home much refreshed.

After the loss of my wife in 1968, I needed help with the upkeep of the house. I ran a newspaper ad for a helper, and among the many applicants, there was a young Korean boy whom I employed—"on approval." His cooking repertoire was limited, but he was eager to please and quick to learn. John Haan had graduated from high school in Korea, and his English left much to be desired. Night classes helped him to improve his language skills and prepared him to attend classes at the University of California, Los Angeles. I eventually came to regard John as my foster son.

While attending a Korean Christian church, John met a lovely Korean girl, Hei Soon, who was a registered nurse. While in Korea, she had been recruited by an American representative whose job it was to find a number of Korean college girls who could be trained as nurses to help solve the critical shortage of nurses in the United States. John and Hei Soon hit it off well from the start, and after several months dating, they became engaged. Later, I was privileged to provide a nice wedding for them.

Both John and Hei Soon liked the idea of making their home in Santa Barbara, and Hei Soon was offered a good nursing position at a hospital in Santa Barbara. In due time, they were blessed with a healthy baby boy, John, Jr. Two years later, they had a second son, David.

At UCLA, John met the sons of successful Korean fathers who wanted their sons to have an American education. When the fathers came to visit their sons, John met them and brought a few of the outstanding fathers home for me to meet. Since most of them spoke English, our times together were quite interesting.

I showed the fathers around and took them for tours of my La Brea museum. One father, a Mr. Kim, had just returned from Arabia where he lived for several years during the oil boom— when money rolled in from the high price of oil. The Arabs were eager to improve their country, and Kim, a building contractor, was able to get large, profitable contracts for huge projects. He operated more profitably than most contractors, who had difficulty getting help. As soon as Kim would get a contract, he would notify his agent in Korea to recruit experienced craftsmen with the various skills required for the job. The workers were transported by the hundreds in chartered ships from Korea to Saudi Arabia. Because of this, Kim's labor cost was drastically reduced, and that made his projects extremely profitable.

On his stop-off to see his son at UCLA, Mr. Kim was hoping to buy each of his children a parcel of California property. He asked if I would help him. I was able to suggest the areas I felt would appreciate in value, and he was eager to buy on my advice. In addition, I suggested that he try to not appear too anxious to buy and when quoted a price, to always offer less. However, if a property appealed to him, in his enthusiasm he would become excited and say, "I'll take it!" And he did. Parcel after parcel, he purchased the real estate for his various children—children by his first, second and third wives. Before leaving, he asked me to be sure to see him if I ever came to Korea. I promised I would.

Another father was a four-star general in the Korean army and an exceptionally likable man. I enjoyed making General Lee's visit pleasant, and, of course, I also took him for a tour of my museum. He was very impressed by the exhibits and told me how he wished that Korea could find someone who could breathe new life into their museums.

As General Lee was leaving, he expressed his desire for me to visit his country. I answered, "That it would be nice. Hopefully, someday I can."

Within a month after his return home, I received a fat envelope from Korea. Enclosed was an invitation from the Korean government to travel to their country for a week as their guest, all expenses paid. In a separate envelope was a round-trip, first-class Korean Airline ticket, together with hotel reservations and a booklet, in English, outlining a schedule of what I could see each day while in Korea. Of course, I made plans to take advantage of this magnificent invitation!

I decided that I would need an interpreter, so I asked if I might bring with me my foster son's wife, Hei Soon. "Yes, you may," they answered and mailed another first-class, round-trip ticket for her. So Hei Soon and I flew in style on a sleek Korean Airline Boeing 747, with lovely stewardesses and the best of food.

I thought that, upon our arrival in Korea, we would take a taxi to our hotel. Imagine my surprise when General Lee and several other dignitaries were waiting to greet us with a special chauffeured car for my personal use—complete with a white-gloved driver and footman. At my side was a colonel assigned to act as my official interpreter, and ahead of us was a lead car with a siren!

At the Shela Hotel, the finest in the city, a two-bedroom suite had been reserved for us. In the living room was a huge basket of flowers and another lovely basket of every imaginable kind of fresh fruit. My interpreter suggested that after a rest, we would go to one of their finest restaurants for dinner. We did—and it was indeed very good. The next morning, we followed the agenda as suggested in the booklet and did some sight-seeing.

The following day, they had arranged for us to be seated in the official box to review the annual military parade. Although people had stood for hours along the streets to see the parade, our car was privileged to drive on a closed-off street, right up to the stairway of the official platform where the top "military brass" and diplomats were seated. The parade began at once, and I was indeed impressed with the endless rows of handsome young men in smart uniforms marching in perfect precision, followed by bands and military equipment, including tanks and big guns.

Each day of our visit was fascinating. We toured museums where the directors were waiting to guide us through and relate their historical stories. On one of the days, my entourage and I were flown by helicopter to the DMZ—the Demilitarized Zone between North and South Korea—where we met the men in charge of the 40,000 American troops stationed there. We were shown the tunnel that the North Koreans used to try to enter South Korea. We also could see the dividing fence where the North Koreans had attached loudspeakers that played American jazz and over which a young woman would periodically ask in English, "Aren't you fellows worried about what your girl friends are doing while you're over here wasting your time?"—and other psychological propaganda... anything to discourage our boys and make them want to return home.

The next day, we visited the Korean military academy—"Eastpoint," if you will. It was a very impressive place, with hundreds of sharp young men in uniform. I was invited to review the troops, after which I sat at lunch with the top military leaders. To make Hei Soon comfortable, General Lee's wife sat next to her, and they chatted in Korean. Fortunately for me, most of the senior officers spoke English, having been trained in the United States.

At the time of our departure from the academy, I was presented with a complete cadet parade uniform, including a hat with plume, a sword and a pair of white shoes. That night, we were taken to their finest nightclubs as a diversion after the day's sight-seeing.

On another day, the same big helicopter flew my entourage on a tour over the rice paddies, fish ponds, picturesque villages and magnificent buildings, some centuries old. Each day was filled with interesting things to see and do, and each evening I had a hot sauna bath, followed by young women giving me a body massage and walking with their bare feet up and down my spine!

The week ended all too soon. Again the group of military leaders accompanied us to the airport, where we departed for home with our arms full of farewell gifts. When I returned home and had to open the door for myself, it took a little getting used to!

A group of handicapped children in front of my
museum, 1990

CHAPTER FOURTEEN

S hortly after I first arrived in Los Angeles in 1917, I learned that there was a place called the "tar pits," where fantastic fossils had been discovered. I took a streetcar to the Wilshire Boulevard site but found only holes where the fossils had been removed. I then had to take a bus to the Museum of Natural History in Exposition Park, where the fossils had been placed and a few had been assembled. Sure enough, in a wing of the museum, I was awed to find the skeletons of prehistoric elephants, camels, 10-foot-high sloths, lions larger than those in a circus, saber-toothed cats and a variety of other wild animals and birds.

I was captivated by the thought that these beasts actually existed right here in Southern California in the dim past. What a heritage it was! And what a wonderful attraction they would be, if the ancient finds could be exhibited in a facility on the site where they were discovered. That was my dream!

Of course, I could do nothing about it at the time. However, a half century later, things were quite different, and I decided to investigate the possibility of creating a museum at the tar pits with the discovered specimens exhibited in an interesting manner. Such an attraction, I felt, would not only be of interest to school children and all Californians, but also to out-of-state visitors and even people from abroad. A fantastic heritage like the specimens from the tar pits deserved a fitting setting.

I learned that the tar pits were part of a 23-acre parcel of land given to Los Angeles County by Alan Hancock in 1916. This was before the city limits were extending out to include the parcel.

The county, in turn, assigned the responsibility of the tar pits to the Los Angeles County Museum. The museum staff had removed tons of fossil bones from the tar pits and taken them to the museum in Exposition Park. Their experts assembled a number of specimens by the old method of using plumbing pipes as supports. The skeleton of a 9,000-year-old woman had been recovered and was exhibited on a sheet of plywood. The public came to see the ancient fossils, but the crude displays didn't excite the children nor incline the adults to return.

I felt confident that both children and adults would be interested if the specimens were displayed in an interesting manner in a facility on the site where they were found. Therefore, I presented a rendering of my ideas of a proper museum, together with an offer to build the facility as a gift to the people of Los Angeles, to the museum board. They liked the idea, and two of the members, Dr. Richard Call and Ed Harrison, were sufficiently enthused to arrange a meeting for me with the Los Angeles County Board of Supervisors. The supervisors also liked my idea, and supervisors Ed Edelman and Kenneth Hahn were so pleased that they persuaded the board to give me a permit to build my museum at the tar pits with the understanding that, when completed, I would turn over the keys of the new facility to the Los Angeles County Museum as "their child." In order to give the supervisors peace of mind, I posted a one-million-dollar bond guaranteeing that I would complete the project and pay all the bills.

After considering various architects, I gave the work to Frank Thornton and Willis Fagan because they came up with the concept that I felt was right for the subject—and they impressed me as being conscientious, ingenious and capable.

With their help, I awarded the construction contract, and as soon as our plans were approved, we got the building permit and started construction. To build a structure *over* the tar pits, with the oily ooze and methane gas seeping up, was indeed a challenge. Fortunately, the architect's engineer knew how to cope with the problem. Immediately after the ground had been cleared, a preliminary slab of two-inch-thick cement was poured over the area where the structure would stand. A heavy reinforced plastic sheet was then laid over the entire floor area; this would prevent the methane gas from seeping through the 24 inches of additional cement. For this to work, it was necessary that the pouring of the cement be continuous and that there be no cold joints.

We had only started, however, when a group of picketers showed up with placards reading, "Stop this man before he destroys our park." Then they placed a woman at the park entrance, and she asked people to sign a petition to stop "this fellow Page" from robbing the laboring people of their recreational park.

Realizing how serious an interruption of the cement-pouring would be, my stomach began to churn. Luckily, Supervisor Ed Edelman came to our rescue. He ordered the group to come to his office where he persuaded them to not interfere. They didn't reappear, and the slab was poured without further interruption—and without a cold joint.

By having a trailer-office on the job, I was able to supervise every step of the construction, and I was pleased with the good work and the quality of the construction. We completed the building on schedule, and I delivered the keys to Giles Mead, Director of the Museum of Natural History, so that his museum staff could install the fossils and complete the La Brea museum as originally planned.

A mother and baby mastodon outside of my museum

To my surprise and shock, Mead told me that he was sorry but they didn't have the money to finish the project; therefore, the building would have to stand vacant for awhile. This was unacceptable to me. I said, "No, I didn't build this museum to stand vacant! If you can't do the exhibit work, I suppose I'll have to do it."

It was Mead's turn to be shocked, because he couldn't conceive of how an inexperienced man, who just happened to have been lucky in the world of commerce, could ever put together a museum that wouldn't be a source of embarrassment to the Museum of Natural History. Nevertheless, when he couldn't do the job, I took over.

I inquired as to who was the best person in the country to assemble fossils using the new method of "invisible" steel rods (a method that allows the specimens to appear as though they are standing without support). I learned that there was a Dr. Jenson on the faculty of Brigham Young University in Provo, Utah, who was one of the very best. I contacted the dean and asked if I could arrange for Jenson to get a leave of absence. After considerable negotiations, Jenson came with his crew and stayed until all the specimens were properly assembled. In addition to the steel supports, the ancient fossils were suspended by small cables from the ceiling to prevent them from falling when earthquakes occur. Dr. Jenson did a superb job, and I was glad to bestow a token of my appreciation on Brigham Young University.

I couldn't find a muralist to my liking in California, but I heard about an exceptional couple residing in Pennsylvania. Jerome and

Elma Connelly worked for several big eastern museums doing just the kind of work I wanted. We talked on the telephone, and I asked if they would be interested in painting the murals in my new museum. "Oh, no," they replied. "We have all the work we want right here."

"Well," I said, "how would you like to come to California as my guests, all expenses paid, to see my museum—with no obligation to stay?" They came, and when I saw their portfolio, I was determined that they do the murals. By supplying them with the use of a car, an apartment, a television—plus a fat contract—I was able to convince them to stay. They completed all the murals to my satisfaction. As it turned out, Elma Connelly was also very capable in helping to put together dioramas. Needless to say, this worked out to be a very beneficial association.

Thanks to the expertise of architects Frank Thornton and Willis Fagan, the general layout and design of the George Page Museum exhibits command the admiration of museum experts. I had to search for the other craftsmen I needed, and some proved to be outstanding. A young University of Southern California art major, Hollis Cotton, proved to be invaluable as my assistant, and little by little, with lots of patience, the project was completed.

To make the museum more understandable to guests, I had a short film made that explains the discoveries and answers questions about the unique tar pits. By having two minitheaters in the museum, no one ever has to wait long to see the show. The audio-visual equipment proved to be very costly, but I felt the cost was justified. Seeing the film adds interest and enjoyment to visitors' tours.

Not a single dinosaur bone has ever been found in the state of California. The reason is that California was under water 65 million years ago, in the age of dinosaurs. Consequently, there are no dinosaur exhibits in my museum. But because children are so interested in dinosaurs, I arranged to have a special theater that shows dinosaur films continuously. It's a very popular feature with the kids. Children also love the exhibit where they can actually pull metal rods up from the tar, to experience what it would be like to be caught in the sticky stuff.

With the help of Walt Disney imagery genius Yale Gracey, I arranged to show the skeleton of the 9,000-year-old woman standing in a glass case. And as you watch her, she changes to a pretty native girl with long black hair—I like to believe that's how she looked in life! The illusion is done with mirrors and lights, and the children love it. Speaking of the Walt Disney Company, a young man who has been very helpful to me is Keith Kambak, an executive with Disney. He's one of the very successful and talented children of my longtime business associate and personal friend, Maynard Kambak. Maynard's lovely wife, Patty, is the epitome of "the perfect mother." No wonder all of their six children are successful.

Giving Prince Charles a tour of my museum

April 13, 1977, the opening night of the museum, was a gala occasion, with the cream of Los Angeles society anxious "to see what George Page had created." There wasn't one word of criticism from anyone—not even from the media.To the contrary, I was showered with praise and compliments, and everyone seemed to be pleased with the project.

Since the opening in 1977, several million visitors from the United States and many foreign countries have toured the museum. They are fascinated because it's different. Prince Charles of England was a visitor, and I had the privilege of being his host for the afternoon. Being a paleontology buff, Prince Charles took a special interest in the exhibits, and it was indeed a pleasure for me to give him a tour. Many distinguished guests have followed him, and all have been very favorably impressed. A number have sent me letters extolling the museum. The hundreds of letters that I've received from school children are a great source of joy to me, because they assure me that the museum has lived up to my fondest hopes. It is giving pleasure to both young and old and has proven to be one of my most rewarding philanthropic projects. Every time I see school buses lining the block by the museum, bringing school children from far and near, I get a deep feeling of satisfaction—and I know my time and efforts were justified.

In 1988, I attended the Olympics in Seoul, Korea, and my friends General Lee and Mr. Kim, the fantastically successful building contractor, were on hand to greet me. They certainly made me welcome in their country, with a special French restaurant dinner...and fruit and flowers again waiting in my suite. This time, I was accompanied to Korea by Dr. Charles Runnels, chancellor of Pepperdine University.

I made it a point to visit Mr. Kim in his penthouse office on the top floor of his high-rise bank building. That night, he arranged for Dr. Runnels and me to be taken to his magnificent country estate where he was giving a royal reception for several Arab princes that he had business dealings with in Saudi Arabia. For this occasion, he didn't "spare the horses," as the old saying goes. There was a large orchestra, a dance floor on the grass and one group of entertainers after another. It was a sparkling evening. I was entertained by a 19-year-old "geisha doll" who danced beautifully and was most interesting. Being fed with chopsticks took a little getting used to, but the graceful way the Korean geisha girls go about it made it easy to take! The food was the very best: sea food, steaks—everything a person could imagine—everything from baby octopus to little roasted birds no larger than humming birds...come to think of it, maybe they *were* humming birds.

The following day, we attended the opening ceremonies of the 1988 Olympics, and that was beyond a doubt one of the most spectacular events of my lifetime. The Koreans had everything perfectly arranged, and the sight of so many well-mannered young people of different nationalities, all competing for medals, was stunning. The crowds were well-managed, and by limiting the use of cars to those with license plates ending in an even digit one day, and those ending in an odd digit the next day, the number of cars at any one time was cut in half. Consequently, there was no congestion, and everything ran incredibly smoothly.

All athletic facilities were completed in advance of and especially for the Olympics, and I couldn't help but be amazed by the planning that went into each one. For example, the swimming pool not only enabled a camera to record every stroke above water, but a long glass window below the waterline enabled another camera to record every stroke underneath. Immediately after the swimmers crossed the pool, we saw every stroke above and below water on a large television screen in a slow motion replay.

CHAPTER FIFTEEN

U pon my return home from the Olympics in Korea, I concentrated on ways to make my museum more inviting. Hundreds of children were being brought from towns all over the state to visit the Page Museum. After the long bus ride, they were often hungry and thirsty. But there was no place to get a snack nearby. So, I decided to do something about the problem of providing snacks for the museum visitors.

I was opposed to serving food or drinks in the museum because of possible damage to the carpeting. However, a snack bar located outside would solve the problem and would be very convenient for the guests. Therefore, I built and stocked a modest snack bar under the observation deck, on the edge of the lake in front of the museum. I persuaded my foster son, John, to operate the snack bar because I knew he could do it in the manner I thought it should be done. John donned an apron and opened for business! The stand has now been open for a number of years. John has kept it open every day that the museum was open, and it has proved to be a blessing for the hungry and thirsty children, as well as a convenience for adult guests.

John Jr., now 13 years of age, attends a private school in Carpinteria, California, and is among the top of his class. He plays the piano for recitals, has become one of the school's best tennis players and is an outstanding swimmer. Young David, at 6, plays the violin and shows promise for becoming a good student—and another credit to his parents.

They both call me "Grandpa," and I like that. However, in stores and public places when ladies hear the children call me "Grandpa," they give me a "look"—and I somehow know they are thinking, "The old goat must have taken an Asian bride!"

After my museum was completed, I noticed that a line of trees along Wilshire Boulevard prevented people passing by from realizing that a museum was there. Not long ago, I decided to do something about the situation. A tall sign or billboard was out of the question. Therefore, I came up with the idea of a large cement monument with an 11-foot-long saber-toothed cat on top, that displayed a message reading,

GEORGE C. PAGE MUSEUM
TAR PIT DISCOVERIES

The monument is very eye-catching, with a half block of landscaping around it, including attractive shrubs and flowers. At night, it's especially attractive, illuminated by two powerful floodlights. I feel confident that the monument will substantially increase the interest and attendance at the museum. My personal effort and expense will then be justified.

Among our private universities in the United States, many have attractive campuses. However, I believe none surpasses the 830-acre setting of the Pepperdine University campus located on a hillside in Malibu, overlooking the blue Pacific Ocean. This beautiful and unique setting naturally creates an atmosphere that is relaxing and conducive to learning. The limited enrollment enables students to get acquainted and form lifetime friendships. Also, the university's high standards of academic achievement and the dedicated faculty and staff help to explain why the graduating students are so clean-cut, clear-eyed, well prepared, articulate and ready to meet whatever lies ahead with enthusiasm.

I know from personal experience the handicap of not having formal training in business. This gave me the incentive to provide a substantial endowment at Pepperdine to assist qualified students of limited means to have important scholarship aid.

During my many years in business, I never thought of any employee as being of any particular race, creed or color. I communicated with them on a common level, as equal human beings. One of the many memorable relationships that I recall was with Barney Jones, an African-American employee who started with me as a young man. After 30 years in my employ, he developed an ailment that handicapped him in doing his work. I gave him a paid retirement until he died. After his death, his son sent me a very beautiful and heartwarming letter expressing his deep appreciation for what I had done for his father throughout the years.

For my 90th birthday, on June 25, 1991, the various organizations I have helped wanted to give me special birthday parties to show their appreciation. ChildHelp USA reserved the Beverly Hilton Hotel ballroom, well in advance, for approximately 750 guests on the evening of April 1. Their party experts, Mrs. Fred (June Haver) MacMurray and Mrs. Happy (Frances) Franklin, left no stone unturned to make the occasion a blockbuster—and how they succeeded! There was excellent entertainment by Hollywood celebrities of yesterday and today; a gourmet dinner; a dance orchestra; and a special feature with Ginger Rogers in person, showing clips from her outstanding films. Many Hollywood personalities were there. I thanked everyone for the very successful birthday party. My only concern, I told them, was that, by publicizing the fact that it was my 90th birthday, they had put me in the "dog house" with my lady friends. You see, I had been telling them that I was 69!

ChildHelp USA is certainly doing a great service, helping abused children across America. When I first met the co-founders, Sara O'Meara and Yvonne Fedderson, I was very impressed by how their organization began and by the good work they have accomplished. It has been, and is, a pleasure for me to give them a helping hand!

A short time later, Pepperdine University followed with an equal number of guests in the same beautiful Hilton ballroom, paying tribute to me on my 90th birthday. Pepperdine didn't spare any effort either and put on a terrific party. It began with a magnificent pre-dinner spread of bountiful hors d'oeuvres displayed with a spectacular, huge sculptured ice figure. A gourmet dinner followed. The dinner table centerpieces were magnificent displays of flowers and fresh fruits, in keeping with my early Mission Pak business. Pepperdine's talented students staged a very professional production depicting the events that led up to founder George Pepperdine establishing his college (which, of course, is now a university).

Another highlight of the party was when the Pepperdine chorus sang a rendition of my Mission Pak radio advertising jingle. It brought back many memories to me. Then a very unique birthday cake, in the form of a crate of oranges, was presented to me—and even the crate replica was edible!

The program continued with words of welcome from the chancellor, Dr. Charles Runnels, and a most inspiring talk by Pepperdine's president, Dr. David Davenport, who had just returned from a sabbatical leave in England and France. President Davenport paid tribute to me by saying many nice things, then went on to deliver his inspiring speech.

The Los Angeles County Museum of Natural History also staged a delightful birthday party for me at my Page Museum. Present from the Museum were Dr. Craig C. Black, director; Mr. Mark A. Rodriguez, chief deputy director; along with several staff members. There were also distinguished city of Los Angeles guests including Supervisor Edelman and Councilman Ferraro. Again, I can only say how very much I enjoyed and shall always treasure the memory of the occasion.

The House Ear Institute staged their party for me at the lovely Beverly Hills home of Mrs. Theodore E. (Suzanne) Cummings, wife of the former Ambassador to Austria appointed by President Ronald Reagan. Violins greeted the guests upon arrival, and after a magnificent buffet dinner, singing musicians played and strolled among the distinguished guests. To see and visit with Dr. Howard House and to meet and greet his son, Dr. John House, was a pleasure, especially knowing that John will be president of the institute, which is probably one of the world's most advanced ear-problem institutions.

For a period of years, I've been very interested in the remarkable work the House Ear Institute has been doing for people of all ages with hearing problems. Besides helping the afflicted, they train hundreds of otologists from all over the world in their new clinic. In this way, the doctors can take home the latest in methods for caring for patients with hearing problems. Many children, in particular, as well as people of all ages, have benefited from advanced techniques in surgery. I consider it a privilege to be able to support a cause so deserving.

Children's Hospital also honored me. Staged in the banquet room of the internationally known Chasen's Restaurant, they provided for me an outstanding birthday party under the expert guidance of Anne Wilson.

Again, many distinguished guests and old friends from years gone by were there to honor me. It was superbly organized, from special hors d'oeuvres to an elegant dinner, which was prepared by Chasen's—as only Chasen's can. The many complimentary speeches given on my behalf served to reassure me that what I had done for Children's Hospital was remembered and greatly appreciated by the administration, staff and friends. What I've done for Children's Hospital has been a labor of love!

In addition to all these large gatherings, there were several dinner birthday parties given for me in private homes by family and friends. Of course, I'm deeply grateful for all the efforts the various organizations expended to make my 90th birthday an event of a lifetime. In my mind's eye, I'll continue to see and relive the great honors I have been paid.

A group of children tour my museum

CHAPTER SIXTEEN

I understand that criminals sometimes have an urge to visit the scenes of their crimes! Well, I had a similar urge to visit the scenes of my various projects. So, I asked my driver, Alberto Flamenco, to take me first to the south part of Los Angeles, around 110th and Main streets. There I saw a number of the cottages I built some 60 years ago. I was surprised to see how well the cottages looked—all occupied and bringing, I was told, over $300 a month in rent.

Continuing my journey of reflections, we next traveled on to the corner of El Segundo and Crenshaw boulevards, in the city of Hawthorne. It was here that I bought land and added two feet of fill dirt to create an industrial park. The land is still covered by the industrial buildings that I built around 40 years ago. Here too, the buildings looked good and are, without exception, occupied. In fact, some are still occupied by my first tenants, mostly the large aerospace companies.

Next, we drove to Fullerton, California, and there again, the brick and tilt-up industrial buildings I had built looked good and were all occupied by leasing tenants. Some of the buildings were on George Page Street, a name I gave at the time of subdividing.

We also visited the area around 33rd and Main streets in Los Angeles to inspect the building that had been my packing house and headquarters for Mission Pak. The 90,000-square-foot structure looked different because all the windows had been covered to create one gigantic block, and the building had been painted a light grey. Seeing no windows on 33rd Street, we drove around to the 32nd Street side, and there I spotted an open door. I took the liberty of entering and was greeted by a Korean security officer. I introduced myself as the former owner of the property, and I told him I was just curious as to the present use of the building.

The young man was then very nice and invited me to look around. I was shocked and overwhelmed by the change. All my lofts and partitions had been removed and in the one enormous room, approximately 600 women were operating power sewing machines, making men's pants by the thousands, for some big chain store. A Korean gentleman was operating the business and appeared well organized.

We drove on to 9th Street in Los Angeles where I operated my Star Auto Body business for several years. The original building had been torn down, so there was nothing familiar about this property except the address: 810 East 9th Street.

Then, to complete our tour, we drove to where I had built my English-style residence in 1927, overlooking Silver Lake. We stopped on Kenilworth Avenue in front of the house so that I could see it to advantage. At that point, the owner came out to inquire if we were looking for someone. I explained how, 65 years ago as a young man of 27, I had built the house.

"Well, do come in!" said the owner.

I accepted the kind invitation and was happy to see how well the property had been taken care of. I then met the other young man, joint owner of the property, and he, too, was eager to show me both upstairs and downstairs. The two young men expressed their love for the house, and it was evident, because they were taking wonderful care of it and of the garden and pool. I asked if they had any questions about it, because I was familiar with nearly every nail in the building.

"Yes," they said. "We love to use the three fireplaces, but the ash-drops are clogged."

"Well," I said, "look at the base of the brick chimney under the house for the little cast iron door. Open it and rake out the ashes and your ash-drops will function satisfactorily." They were delighted to know this, and before I left, they invited me to stay for lunch!

Last spring, when I wanted to visit my French friends, I boarded a Boeing 747 at Los Angeles International Airport in the evening.

After a "Diamond Jim Brady" dinner, I stretched out, had a good night's sleep and awakened the next morning at the Paris airport, very relaxed and comfortable.

The city of Paris looked pretty much the same. However, a number of new things have been added. For example, there is the new Grand Arche, a colossal structure in the shape of an arch, with 26,000 square feet of office space. The French debated the project for years and finally selected an architect from Denmark, Johan Otto Van Spreckelsen, and completed the building. The new opera house is spectacular, too, but personally, I still like the old one better, with all its "gingerbread."

An Asian-American architect, Mr. Pei, has solved the space problem at the Louvre by excavating an underground area the size of a football stadium. Visitors now enter a glass pyramid at ground level and descend by escalator to the huge waiting room with a number of ticket windows for the different attractions. They then take the stairs to the marbles, paintings and other art exhibits. The Louvre itself has been completely remodeled so that everything is displayed to the best advantage, with good lighting effects.

The high add-on tax, plus the tax from gasoline (which sells for about $5 per gallon), have provided the means for many improvements in France, including a generous health plan, old-age pension and only modest tuition charges for their fine universities. The sales tax is included in everything one buys, but sales tax is never mentioned to the retail purchaser!

One of the most memorable and outstanding days during my recent visit to France was the day I visited Chartres Cathedral. Although I had visited many of the fabulous and beautiful cathedrals on my previous trips to France, Chartres Cathedral impressed me as being very special.

Following the destruction by fire of the former church in 1194, the present replacement was actually built and completed in only 30 years—a most remarkable accomplishment when you consider how most cathedrals took centuries to build.

Both the fine sculpturing and magnificent stained glass windows of Chartres Cathedral are in remarkably good condition and obviously were executed by exceptionally fine and gifted craftsmen. The sculpturing and stained glass windows, of course, were designed to teach the people of the Middle Ages about the Virgin Mary and about Jesus Christ, His followers and the miracles He performed. It was an encyclopedia of life and faith.

The shafts of multicolored lights, shining through these magnificent stained glass windows, create a magical atmosphere. Then, when the powerful organ plays or accompanys the large choir and the aroma of the incense permeates the sanctuary, it literally transports the visitor's awareness into a higher realm of consciousness. I departed on cloud nine!

After making the rounds of the outstanding, fabulous eating places in Paris, we visited the old market where the Pied de Cachon has been in business for more than 50 years. I could hardly wait to taste their speciality—the French delicacy of pigs feet! They boil the feet in vegetable stock until the fat comes out and the meat is as tender as a lady's heart. After they are drained, they roll them in egg and bread crumbs and then bake them to form a toasted crust. When you bite into one of those succulent morsels, your taste buds turn somersaults of ecstasy.

At the end of my two-week stay, I returned home with a heavy heart, but a light pocketbook.

I'm often asked, "To what do you attribute your success?" First, I usually say that I knew what I wanted and I was willing to work hard to achieve it. Second, I realized that well-being is very important if a person is serious about getting ahead in life. And third, I avoided harmful habits and, very importantly, the wrong kind of friends.

I've written this book in the hope that it will make at least some young people understand that it isn't necessary to be born with a silver spoon in your mouth to have a fair chance in life. It's difficult to conceive of one with poorer prospects for success than myself. With an average constitution and only a grammar school education, I was forced to shift for myself at age 16. I made my way in a state where I didn't know a single person, and yet I've done quite well and experienced much success in my business endeavors and earned that wonderful sense of peace and tranquility of mind.

What I *did* have was strong determination—a goal—to be financially independent and successful. I focused my thoughts on that. And I wasn't afraid to work hard. I was self-disciplined, and I had strong faith that I would be successful in "this thing called life."

And so can you. It's worth the effort. Just realize that it all depends on one person—YOU! Most people would *like* to be successful, but that's not enough. You must discipline yourself and be *determined*. It's not easy in the beginning. I held down two jobs and worked 16 hours a day until I got my start towards becoming successful in life. I realized that any venture I undertook would require capital, so I concentrated on that objective until I had the means to begin a modest business. From one little store, the business grew to where I operated more than a hundred retail stores and employed more than a thousand employees.

I suggest that a person always aim for the best and most efficient way of living and doing. For instance, each morning after my two-mile walk and my morning regimen, in a pocket-size notebook, I list things "To Do" that day. The following day, I check my list, rewrite what I didn't complete and add to the new list for that day. By this simple and easy method, things get done in a surprisingly effortless way. In addition, I've found that having a place for everything and putting it back into place after use has saved me much time and frustration.

I have followed Shakespeare's advice on borrowing and lending. He wrote, "Loan oft loses both itself and friend." Consequently, when a dear friend or valued employee has asked for an emergency loan, I've explained that I don't make "loans," but, I say, "I do sympathize with you and will make you a 'gift' of half the amount you asked for." In this way, I save their friendship, avoid the disagreeable task of collecting and save half the amount for which they asked.

Many friends and acquaintances have asked to what I attribute my longevity and, most importantly, the exceptional energy and good health that I've enjoyed. I believe that the primary contributor to my years of good health and well-being is self-discipline. Books on health, diet and exercise have helped me to lead a sensible, well-balanced lifestyle. They taught me what to avoid and what contributes to illnessess and premature aging. Somewhere among my readings, I was very impressed with the following saying:

"Self-discipline can be just as self-satisfying as self-indulgence—and infinitely *more* rewarding."

I have adhered to that principle throughout my lifetime. And, yes, it has been rewarding, indeed!

POSTSCRIPT

My dear friend Catherine Corday Singer was one of those who thought I should write a book of my experiences.

I finally got around to taking pen in hand, and thanks to Catherine's encouragement and invaluable assistance, my autobiography is now completed.

I finished writing it after my ninety-first birthday on June 25th, 1992. That freed me to leave for the Barcelona Olympics in Spain, which I greatly wanted to attend.

To give my friends peace of mind, I explained I was not going to *compete* in jumping, running, swimming or other events—I would merely be an avid spectator!

Pepperdine University

To all to whom these letters shall come, Greeting
The Regents of the University on the recommendation of the Committee
on Degrees and by virtue of the authority in them vested have conferred upon

George Charles Page

the honorary degree of

Doctor of Laws

with all the Rights, Privileges and Honors thereunto appertaining.

Given at Malibu, California, on August 3, 1970

Chairman, Board of Regents

President and Chief Executive Officer